speaking
in tongues

AN ESSENTIAL GUIDE TO

speaking
in tongues

Ron Phillips

**CHARISMA
HOUSE**

Most Charisma House Book Group products are available at special quantity discounts for bulk purchase for sales promotions, premiums, fund-raising, and educational needs. For details, write Charisma House Book Group, 600 Rinehart Road, Lake Mary, Florida 32746, or telephone (407) 333-0600.

An Essential Guide to Speaking in Tongues
    by Ron Phillips
Published by Charisma House
Charisma Media/Charisma House Book Group
600 Rinehart Road
Lake Mary, Florida 32746
www.charismahouse.com

Cover design by Justin Evans
Design Director: Bill Johnson

Visit the author's website at www.ronphillips.org.

Library of Congress Cataloging-in-Publication Data
Phillips, Ron M.
  An essential guide to speaking in tongues / Ron Phillips. -- 1st ed.
      p. cm.
  Includes bibliographical references (p.   ).
  ISBN 978-1-61638-240-7 (trade paper) -- ISBN 978-1-61638-422-7
(e-book) 1. Glossolalia. I. Title.
  BT122.5.P55 2011
  234'.132--dc22
                        2011005730

12 13 14 15 — 9 8 7 6 5 4 3
Printed in the United States of America

CONTENTS

Come, Holy Ghost, and touch my tongue
As with a living flame;
I want the sanctifying grace
My Savior bids me claim.

Come, Holy Ghost, with sacred fire,
Baptize this heart of mine;
Break every earthly idol down,
And all its dross refine.

I want a self-renouncing will,
That owns His sweet control,
And through my life I want His love;
A ceaseless flood to roll.

Come, Holy Ghost, the blood apply
As Thou hast ne'er before,
That I may shout my Savior's praise
Henceforth and evermore.

Waiting, I am waiting,
For the promise of the Pentecostal shower;
Waiting, I am waiting,
For the promise of Thy wondrous, mighty power.[1]

CHAPTER ONE
The Holy Spirit and His Work

JACK HARRIS HAS an interesting hobby. The eighty-six-year-old pensioner is given a new jigsaw puzzle every year for Christmas. Most of his puzzles take no more than a few months casual work to assemble. He took up this hobby to occupy his time during the winter months, which made working in his garden impossible. In 2002, Jack was given a five-thousand-piece puzzle for Christmas, and this puzzle would prove to be a special challenge.

Jack did not finish the puzzle by spring. He hadn't even finished it by the next Christmas. In fact, this massive puzzle took up residence on Jack's dining room table for over seven years. Upon placing the final piece into its position, Jack stood back to admire his work, and it was then that he noticed the puzzle was missing a piece.

Had the piece been eaten by a dog? Accidentally thrown away? Had it never been in the box to begin with? No one knows. His daughter—who originally gave her father the puzzle—tried to contact the maker of the puzzle to procure a spare piece, but it had taken Jack so long to finish the puzzle that they no longer made it. She said, of her father, "He was just so disappointed when he found one piece was missing. It's sad really because now it will never be complete."

So many churches should feel tremendous sympathy for Jack Harris. You see, they experience the feeling of a missing piece—a missing *person*, really—every day.

The "missing person" in today's church is the Holy Spirit. Though the church confesses the Holy Spirit to be fully God, He is seldom worshiped and often ignored.

The Holy Spirit is the third person of the Godhead. The Holy Spirit did not come into existence on the Day of Pentecost, but He came into prominence. John 7:38–39 is where we are clearly told that at the ascension and glorification of Jesus, the Holy Spirit was to be given or poured out upon the church without measure.

> "He who believes in Me, as the Scripture has said, out of his heart will flow rivers of living water." But this He spoke concerning the Spirit, whom those believing in Him would receive; for the Holy Spirit was not yet given, because Jesus was not yet glorified.

Acts 2 records that remarkable and powerful moment! There were sounds not heard since the Holy Spirit roared over the waters of creation. There were sights eyes had never seen in divided tongues of fire. There was a supernatural miracle of speaking and understanding that took place.

The History of Pentecost

Let's contemplate the history of Pentecost. We have mentioned the events of Pentecost as recounted in Acts 2. This is, in fact, the "Pentecost" that most people think of when hearing the word *Pentecostal*. However, the fact is that Pentecost has a much richer history and meaning.

At the first Passover, the Hebrews made their exodus from slavery in Egypt. Fifty days later this newly emancipated nation sat in the shadow of Mount Sinai. Understand the scene here. It's been almost two months since their liberation, and the children of Israel are becoming frustrated already. Moses descended from Sinai and gave God's commands (not the Ten Commandments yet, but the promises and covenant conditions), and the people willingly agreed. God then tells Moses to inform the people that He wants to speak in such a way that the people can hear God speak for themselves. God gave Moses instructions that the people were to sanctify themselves in a number of ways, and on the third day, which was Pentecost, God would come down upon the mountain and speak. So it was on that third day, the people assembled themselves as God had instructed.

God descended on the mountain, and the people saw fire and heard thunder and the sound of trumpets. According to Exodus 19:16, this sound was so loud that people in the camp trembled. Here, the narrative becomes cloudy if the reader doesn't understand the varieties of Jewish literary approaches. In Exodus 19:19 it says that when Moses spoke, "God answered him by voice." The implication here is that some people heard simply noise (thunder, wind, and trumpets), and some heard God's voice. Chapter 19 continues on with Moses going up the mountain to speak to God. Then in the last verse of chapter 19, it says that Moses went back down the mountain to speak with the people.

Now watch how chapter 20 opens: "And God spoke all these words, saying..." What we have here is a classic

Eastern literary device—similar to an ellipsis—where, essentially, the first verse of chapter 20 (remember, chapters and verses didn't exist in the Hebrew text) is the continuation of the story that is begun in Exodus 19:19. So, when it says there that "God answered him by a voice," the next thing to happen chronologically is Exodus 20:1.

So what was it that God wanted the Israelites to hear? Read Exodus 20:2–17, and you see that the words God spoke to the Israelites were the Ten Commandments. In short, God wanted His word to live inside them! But the people were too afraid. Again, some heard only rumblings and loud noises. "Then they said to Moses, 'You speak with us, and we will hear. But let not God speak with us, lest we die'" (Exod. 20:19).

Fast-forward approximately fifteen hundred years to the events of Acts chapter 2. The apostles and other disciples are gathered in the upper room. Christ Himself has sanctified them and told them to wait. Let's take a close look at what the Greek text tells us.

> Then there appeared to them divided tongues, as of fire, and one sat upon each of them.
> —ACTS 2:3

Take note here of the word *sat*. This word in the Greek is *kathizo*, which can mean to sit or hover, but in its form here it means to dwell. So this fire came down to dwell in the believers there.

> And they were all filled with the Holy Spirit and began to speak with other tongues [in other languages], as the Spirit gave them utterance.
> —ACTS 2:4

Without making the attempt to become overly exhaustive, let's just look here at the words "began to speak." It is beyond a question of debate that the people there were saying something. But what?

> And when this sound occurred, the multitude came together, and were confused, because everyone heard them speak in his own language.
> —ACTS 2:6

A certain multitude of people heard these men and women speaking in their, the hearers', own language. The implication in verses 6–12 is that various hearers heard various speakers in their, the hearers', native language. This seems to make short work of those who say that the *glossa* (tongues) given on Pentecost was an earthly language. But is there more evidence to support this?

> Others mocking said, "They are full of new wine."
> —ACTS 2:13

Have you ever wondered what these others heard? We have already said that it is beyond debate that those present in the upper room were saying something; so why did some hear their own language and some hear the kind of babbling that would cause them to believe that the disciples were simply drunk on new wine?

Let's compare the two events. At the first Pentecost in Exodus, God tried to place His word in the hearts of His children, but they refused out of fear. The Pentecost of Acts 2 found His children ready to receive. Simply stated, Pentecost, as well as the baptism of the Holy Spirit, is God breaking open the windows of heaven to place the same Spirit that raised Jesus from the dead into the lives of those who are willing to accept it.

Are you willing?

The Curse of Babel

After the Flood, mankind was joined together and united in geography, culture, language, and purpose. Today, this kind of unity is much sought after, but look at what is said in Genesis 11:6 (KJV) regarding this situation:

> And the Lord said, Behold, the people is one, and they have all one language; and this they begin to do: and now nothing will be restrained from them, which they have imagined to do.

The word translated *imagined* has, in the Hebrew, a very negative connotation. The word truly implies plotting or scheming. Essentially, God saw the wickedness in their hearts and saw that the ability of the people to do wickedness was enhanced by their ability to all speak a unified language. So God saw fit to confound their languages and disperse them from that one place.

It is this curse that lasted through the centuries up until the time of Christ. God raised up governments and empires that unified much of the known world. Consider it: at the time of Jesus, the Roman Empire had succeeded the Grecian empire of Alexander the Great, facilitated travel throughout the empire by building roads, and unified the empire's speech by adopting a form of Greek as its common language. This facilitated the spread of the gospel, to be sure, but it was also a physical manifestation of a greater spiritual truth.

At Pentecost the curse of Babel was reversed, and all the nations could hear the good news of Jesus. There was a powerful sermon based upon Old Testament prophecy: "This is what was spoken by the prophet Joel…" (Acts 2:16). The message of Jesus was preached, three thousand received salvation, and the church was born. Acts 2:38 speaks of the gift of the Spirit, but what does the Holy Spirit *do*?

The Work of the Spirit Is Indispensable

A cursory search through Scripture shows us that the Holy Spirit has a place of extreme prominence and significance. We turn the pages of our spiritual history and find that Scripture teaches us that the Holy Spirit:

- Was the agent of Creation (Gen. 1:2)
- Inspired the sacred Scriptures (2 Pet. 1:21)
- Conceived the Lord Jesus in the womb of Mary (Luke 1:35)
- Filled Jesus at His baptism (Matt. 3:16)
- Taught through Jesus (Isa. 61:1; Luke 4:18)
- Raised Jesus from the dead (Rom. 8:11)
- Birthed the church into being (Acts 2)
- Convicts the world of sin, righteousness, and judgment (John 16:7–11)
- Brings the new birth (John 3:5–8)
- Speaks to the church today (Rev. 2–3)

+ Enables us to pray (Rom. 8:26)
+ Makes the Word of God come alive (Heb. 4:12)
+ Makes worship possible (John 4:20–24)
+ Glorifies Jesus (John 16:13–14)

The Work of the Spirit Is Individual

We will discuss this in slightly more detail later, but it is important to note that your experience with the Holy Spirit will be *your* experience. It won't be some pale imitation of the experience had by a loved one, a mentor, or a pastor you admire. God wishes to enable a work in you that can only be done by you! That is one of the many reasons obedience to the call of God is so important. The work God has for you to do is work only you can do. To help the believer accomplish this, God has sent His precious Holy Spirit.

The gift of the Spirit is God Himself indwelling the believer (Acts 2:38). The gifts of the Spirit are the abilities of Jesus manifested through His people. The filling of the Holy Spirit is the action or power of Jesus in and through His people. This is a repeated event. (See Ephesians 5:18.) Primarily the filling is the enabling of the believer to bear witness to Christ. The baptism of the Holy Spirit is the acceptance by Jesus into the realm of the Spirit, especially the body of Christ, the church. This is a once and for all event. (See 1 Corinthians 12:13; Matthew 3:11.) The fruit of the Spirit is the attitude of Jesus demonstrated in the life of the believer. (See Galatians 5:22–23.) The call of the Spirit is the anointing of Jesus sometimes described as the Spirit coming upon (Greek, *epi*, "into") an individual for a special service.

The Work of the Holy Spirit Is Inscrutable!

Make no mistake about this: the Holy Spirit will not be used! Those who think they can live in sin and still flow in the work of the Spirit are headed for disaster. Those who would live without a devotional life are rushing in "where angels fear to tread."

The Holy Spirit will not be managed. The Holy Spirit will never fit into our human mold. He will be in control, or He will not stay. This might seem constricting or even tyrannical to those who do not understand that "where the Spirit of the Lord is, there is liberty" (2 Cor. 3:17).

The Holy Spirit cannot be contained. (See John 3:8.) Like a mighty wind the Spirit of God moves. The hurricane of heaven that roared over creation acts in sovereignty. Like a mighty flooding river the Spirit moves and overflows. Ezekiel 47:1–12 pictures the river of God flowing out of the temple. Jesus said in John 7:38 that out of the temple of our hearts there could be a river of living water. Like a mighty fire the Holy Spirit of God consumes. Hebrews 12:29 says, "Our God is a consuming fire." To try to contain the Spirit of God is an impossible task! He will break the dam of denomination-alism. He will transform tradition. One might as well try to harness a hurricane or fetter a fire or flood! Beloved, when you receive Jesus Christ, the Holy Spirit comes to live in you. He is the Spirit of the Father and of the Son. He comes to bring gifts, to bear fruit, to fill, to anoint, and to enable. The question to all of us is this: Do you have the Holy Spirit? "If any man have not the Spirit of Christ, he is none of his" (Rom. 8:9, KJV).

The believer is "led by the Spirit of God," and God's Spirit bears witness with the believer's spirit that he is a child of God (Rom. 8:14–16). The Spirit of Christ sends the birthing of "Abba Father" into your hearts (Gal. 4:6). (See also 1 John 3:24; 4:13.) A final question as we open this book on the grace of tongues: Does the Holy Spirit have you?

CHAPTER TWO

The Gift and the Gifts of the Holy Spirit

IT IS IMPORTANT that you understand the difference between the "gift" of the Spirit and the "gifts" of the Spirit. Much confusion abounds in many churches because of this failure in understanding. Also you need to understand the gift of tongues in context with the other gifts.

The gift of the Spirit to the church was given after the ascension and glorification of our Savior. (See John 7:39.) Now the Holy Spirit had been in the world, but now in a new and special way He came to live in the hearts of His people. He came to dwell permanently within us (John 14:16–17, 26). In Acts 2:38 the sinner is commanded to repent, after which the Holy Spirit will be given. The word is singular, *gift*. In Acts 10:45 the gift is seen as given to non-Jews also.

The gift of the Holy Spirit is given to every believer at the moment of conversion. At the moment of conversion you are baptized by the Holy Spirit (Acts 2:38; 1 Cor. 12:13). This means that you are immersed in the Spirit and He in you.

Once we are saved and have the indwelling Spirit, then we may be *filled* with the Holy Spirit. The filling of the Spirit is God's controlling presence in our lives. He will fill only what we yield to Him. We may have the Spirit and yet not be filled with the Spirit.

Now all of this has to do with the "gift" of the Spirit. He comes into our lives to save us, sustain us, and strengthen us.

So, now we understand the singular gift of the Holy Spirit, but the Holy Spirit is also the bestower of gifts to the believer (1 Cor. 12, Rom. 12). These spiritual gifts are endowments of power from God given to us so that we might fulfill the calling of God on our lives. In order to understand the importance of these spiritual gifts, we must first understand the church as the body of Christ.

Paul describes and compares the unity and diversity of the human body to the purpose of spiritual gifts. In this symbolism we learn three important truths.

1. They are divine gifts.

The gifts of the Spirit come from the same source. In 1 Corinthians 12:4–6 we see the source as the triune God. Verse 11 sets forth the fact that these gifts are sovereignly bestowed. God not only gives the gifts, but He also decides who gets which gift. Verse 18 supports this by declaring that God sets the members into the church as it pleases Him.

Spiritual gifts are not natural talents or abilities that you are born with. Those are your natural gifts. Spiritual gifts are the supernatural gifts of God.

2. They are different gifts.

This passage affirms that there are different gifts. In 1 Corinthians 12:4–6 (NIV), the word *different* is used three times. Three very important categories of gifts are listed: motivational gifts, ministry gifts, and manifestation gifts.

The important thing to note is that different gifts are given to different people.

The symbolism of the body holds true here. Every member of the body is different. Paul uses the foot, the hand, the ear, the eye, and the nose. How ridiculous if we were all one foot, eye, ear, hand, or nose. A body is made up of different members.

Each church then has different members with different gifts. When will we learn that we are not all alike, and that it is *in* that diversity—both in our spiritual and social abilities and strengths—that we are best able to function as the body of Christ? Most church problems come because we are intolerant of others with a different motivation than ours. We must learn that all should not be alike. God has made us and gifted us differently. Many quit the church because they can't respond to the differences of others.

3. They are dependent gifts.

Christ's body is unified but not uniform. God has so designed the human body that each member is necessary for it to function properly. The value of a member is in its attachment to the body.

First Corinthians 12:25–26 describes the dependence we ought to have on each other. We ought to care for each other. Suppose my stomach sends a signal to my brain of hunger? My feet carry me to the place where my eyes and nose tell me there is food. My hand grasps a fork and a knife when I see that steak. My hand carries that piece of steak not to my ear or foot or eye, but to that convenient opening in the middle of my face called the mouth. There enamel grinders called teeth chew it up and keep me from choking to death. Next, glands provide liquid so it can be conveyed safely to the stomach where the bloodstream will carry its nutrients to the rest of my body.

Just as the body cares for itself, so the church members are to care for one another, hurt with one another, rejoice with one another. We are the body of Christ, and He is our head. We must move as He directs us. We are not to be divided but be together.

Dangers Associated With the Gifts

There are some interesting but dangerous trends I see in our day.

The neglect of spiritual gifts

God has provided gifts to cause His church to grow. Very few churches operate on the basis of God's gifting. This neglect is one cause of the anemic growth of the Western church.

The fear of spiritual gifts

Some are afraid of the gifts, especially the manifested gifts such as tongues, healing, and miracles. This fear is rooted in control issues. Certainly, excesses can be dealt with in love, but the church must not fear the graces of the Holy Spirit.

The clustering of like gifts

Many churches have incomplete ministries because they have attracted those with like gifts. For instance, a pastor with a strong teaching gift will attract others with the teaching gift. You can end up with a group of well-fed, well-studied teachers and other ministries neglected. If you are one who constantly complains that you are not being "fed," you may be a teacher who needs to be teaching. Babies need to be fed, but mature Christians should be feeding themselves and others. This attitude fails to embrace the gifts of others.

The lack of balance in the body of Christ

Suppose my hands suddenly grabbed a pencil and wrote my eye a note and said, "I am cutting myself off. I am tired of you sitting up there in the head." Why, it would mean the crippling of the body and the death of the hand. We must learn some practical facts about the body of Christ. In summary:

- One part cannot function as the whole (1 Cor. 12:14).
- The task of one cannot be given to another (1 Cor. 12:15–17).
- There are no self-made members (1 Cor. 12:18–20).
- All members are to be directed by the head. Christ is the head of the church.

A young man in my last church cut off three of his fingers while cutting a piece of paneling in a van customizing shop. As he was being rushed to the hospital, he was asked, "Where are the fingers?" A man rushed back to the shop with a bowl of ice, and those fingers were rushed to Birmingham in the ambulance with the young man. Nineteen hours of micro-surgery reattached those fingers. Had those fingers been left in the sawdust of that shop, they would have been useless. They were only good to him if they were attached to his body.

That is why a Christian needs to be in a local body we call the church. He needs to be in his place exercising his gift to the glory of God.

CHAPTER THREE
Speaking in Tongues and Scripture

I**N DEALING WITH** spiritual gifts, the gift of tongues is the elephant in the room. Since the Pentecostal awakening at Azusa Street in Los Angeles, the rebirth of Pentecostalism in the church, and the return of tongues, people have reacted with heated arguments and division.

Speaking in Tongues Defined

The word *tongues* comes from the Greek word *glossa*. *Glossa* is the term for the physical organ and also the word for "languages." In the New Testament you have *glossa*, which means "language," as *laleo*, which means "to speak." Together they form one word in Greek *glossalaleo*, which means "to speak in languages."[1]

Often people equate "speaking in tongues" with the word *glossalalia*. In the New Testament this term could be used for known languages, foreign languages, and angelic languages. (See 1 Corinthians 13:1; Acts 2:4-6.)

According to the *Theological Dictionary of the New Testament* by Gerhard Kittel, the term *glossa* had to do with manner of speech. Also it could refer to a people with their own language.[2]

"The phenomenon of glossalalia is spiritually effected speaking (1 Cor. 14:2) not to men but to God (1 Cor. 14:2, 28), sometimes in the form of praise and thanksgiving and possibly song; in this inspired utterance the mind (*nous* in Greek) is swallowed up so that mysterious word [is] obscure to both speakers and hearers...."[3]

It is important to note that Satan had a counterfeit of this phenomenon. In Greek religion the Cybele cults and the Delphus Phrygia had similar experiences.[4] Such counterfeits should not discourage true Spirit-filled believers.

There are some evidences for ecstatic tongues in the Old Testament. The late Rabbi Getz of Jerusalem shared with Perry Stone that certain ceremonies within the holy of holies included a prayer language.

There is clear evidence of ecstasy among the Old Testament prophets. On occasion the prophets were overcome by the Holy Spirit (1 Sam. 19:20).

The prophets that came to anoint Jehu in place of Jezebel were thought to be babbling madmen (2 Kings 9:11). The great reference tool *The Treasury of Scriptural Knowledge* says this:

> It is probable there was something peculiar in the young prophet's manner and address, similar to the vehement actions sometimes used by the prophets when under the Divine influence, which caused the bystanders to use this contemptuous language.[5]

Isaiah prophesied that God would speak in ecstatic tongues to Israel, a passage later cited by Paul in 1 Corinthians 14:21.

> "For precept must be upon precept, precept upon precept; line upon line, line upon line; here a little, there a little." For with stammering lips and another tongue He will speak to this people.
>
> —ISAIAH 28:10–11

Prophetic singing was witnessed by King Saul, and he began to speak by the Spirit. So utterly affected was he that the Scriptures declared that he was "turned into another man." Also it became a proverb in Israel that Saul was among the prophets (1 Sam. 10:6–12).

The Book of Acts records that the outpouring of the Holy Spirit at Pentecost included manifestations of wind, tongues of fire, and speaking in tongues. According to Kittel, "It is an endowment of the Spirit.... It takes ecstatic forms.... The speakers seem to be like drunkards...."[6]

The same manifestations appear throughout the Book of Acts. In Acts 8:5-7 at Samaria, though tongues are not mentioned, the event has the same element as Pentecost. In Acts 10:45-46 at the home of Cornelius they speak in tongues. Also in Acts 19:6 at Ephesus they speak in tongues. It seems to me that the rhythm of the Holy Spirit follows the missionary mandate of Acts 1:8 when the gospel moved from Jerusalem, to Judea, to Samaria, and to the ends of the earth, fulfilling the Great Commission as found in Mark 16:15–20.

Jesus promised that signs would follow those who believe! Speaking in tongues was included in those signs.

As we move into the epistles of the New Testament, we find that Paul dealt extensively with the gift of tongues in 1 Corinthians. In this letter Paul makes it clear that the gift of tongues includes both languages of the earth and the languages of angels (1 Cor. 13:1). He includes the gift of tongues among other supernatural gifts or *charisma*, to use the Greek term (1 Cor. 12:7–11). In 1 Corinthians 14:2 Paul addresses the element of mystery in the gift of tongues.

I believe that "praying in the Spirit" and "singing in the Spirit" can include the use of tongues.

In 1 Corinthians 14:14–17 praying in the Spirit is viewed differently from prophetic tongues, which must be interpreted. (In a later chapter I will detail the value and difference of both.)

Paul speaks of "singing in the Spirit" in 1 Corinthians 14:15. I believe that "spiritual songs" in Ephesians 5:19 includes songs given by the Spirit in tongues as well as known languages. Prayer in tongues is implied in Paul's closing remarks in Ephesians 6:18.

Surely "all prayer in the Spirit" would include prayer in tongues! I further believe that Paul is exhorting Timothy to speak in tongues in his second letter (2 Tim. 1:6).

Timothy needed to be edified and strengthened. The word *gift* in the above verse is *charismata*. We find this same theme of edification or building up one's faith in Jude 20.

Prayer in the Spirit strengthens believers. Tongues clearly were practiced in the New Testament church.

CHAPTER FOUR
Speaking in Tongues and Jesus Christ

How many times have I heard teachers say Jesus never spoke in tongues? The argument is what those of us who study philosophy call "an argument from silence." Simply, there is no direct evidence saying that Jesus spoke in tongues. I will grant you that, but there is also no evidence that He did not speak in tongues in His prayer life! In fact, I want to share my studies with you of the Greek New Testament and some possibilities about Jesus and tongues that may surprise you.

Before I delve into that part of the study, let me say unequivocally that Jesus endorsed and prophesied about speaking in tongues. In Mark 16:17 He says, "And these signs will follow those who believe: In My name they will cast out demons; they will speak with new tongues."

Here, the Greek word *kairai* is used, which means "new and unusual."

Jesus said new tongues would be a sign that fell on the early believers as they spread the gospel. I recognize that some challenge the last verse of Mark, but the last verses of Mark appear in the majority of manuscripts.[1]

Jesus promised accompanying signs to all who obey the

21

Great Commission. This is verified later in the Book of Hebrews:

> Therefore we must give the more earnest heed to the things we have heard, lest we drift away. For if the word spoken through angels proved steadfast, and every transgression and disobedience received a just reward, how shall we escape if we neglect so great a salvation, which at the first began to be spoken by the Lord, and was confirmed to us by those who heard Him, God also bearing witness both with signs and wonders, with various miracles, and gifts of the Holy Spirit, according to His own will?
>
> —HEBREWS 2:1–4

God verified the words of the gospel by supernatural gifts, signs, and miracles.

Nicodemus and Tongues

What I am about to share with you may be seem unusual. I am not insistent that you agree with me, but I do ask that you receive this research with an open heart. In Jesus's encounter with Nicodemus there is a masterful play on words in the original Greek (John 3:5–8).

In this passage Jesus tells the Old Testament scholar, "You must be born again" (John 3:7). The word *again* translates to Greek *anothen*, which could mean "from above." One cannot access the kingdom of God without a spiritual birth. The spiritual realm opens up to those who have had a second birth by the Holy Spirit.

How does Jesus illustrate this second birth? He uses the

word translated "wind" in our English version. The Greek word normally used for wind is *anemos*. Here the word is *pneuma*. This is the new word translated *Spirit* in John 3:5–8. Literally John 3:8 could read, "The Spirit spirits where He wishes..."

Furthermore, the word translated "sound" is the Greek word *phone*, which means "voiced" or "languages." It is translated by Vincent in his classic word studies the following way, "Thou heardest His voice..."

The Latin Vulgate translates it "hear His voice." Our English word *phonetics* comes from that word. It means *articulated words*.

Could it be that Jesus is telling Nicodemus that the Spirit will articulate phonetically a new language? Could it possibly be translated, "The Spirit blows where it wishes and you hear the articulated language, but cannot tell where it comes from or where it goes. So it is with everyone who is born of the Spirit"?

When Rome brought its kingdom to conquer another land, it brought a language with them—the Greek language, which was the universal language of that day. Could it be that God's kingdom breaking through released "the tongues of angels"?

Certainly Nicodemus would have been present on the Day of Pentecost. What would he have observed and experienced on that day? Nicodemus would have heard "wind blowing" and also a miracle of articulated languages!

Every Jew would have remembered the Old Testament feast day of Pentecost. What happened on that day is history.

God spoke to Moses by "voice" and then descended in power, causing supernatural lightening, thunder, angelic trumpets, and smoke (Exod. 19:16–19). God then gave the law of the commandments. After all this the people "trembled and stood afar off" (Exod. 20:18).

The people told Moses that they didn't want to hear the language of heaven from God's voice (v. 19). Moses tried to assuage these fears so that they could hear God's word themselves (v. 20). Sadly, "The people stood afar off…" (v. 21).

Then the Lord said to Moses, "You have seen that I have talked with you from heaven" (v. 22).

Certainly Nicodemus would have heard the challenge of hearing from heaven and not being afraid of a powerful spiritual breakthrough. Possibly Nicodemus was among the 120 gathered in the upper room on the Day of Pentecost. This time three thousand drew near and received God's voice!

Jesus's Prayer Life

We know that Jesus had a profound prayer life. He would go off for long seasons to pray. He spent forty days fasting and praying before He launched His three-year ministry. He would go pray in the mountains. So profound was His example that the disciples asked Jesus, "Teach us to pray" (Luke 11:1).

It is interesting that the disciples interrupted Jesus's prayer in Luke 11:1. The word *ceased* is the Greek word *pauao*, which means "to cause to pause." Jesus was interrupted.

He then gave the disciples the model prayer:

> So He said to them, "When you pray, say: Our Father in heaven, hallowed be Your name. Your kingdom come. Your will be done on earth as it is in heaven. Give us day by day our daily bread. And forgive us our sins, for we also forgive everyone who is indebted to us. And do not lead us into temptation, but deliver us from the evil one."
>
> —LUKE 11:2–4

Notice that the prayer for kingdom and power and glory is not in Luke. Instead Jesus moves from the pattern of prayer to persistence in prayer. He tells the parable of the friend at midnight.

> And He said to them, "Which of you shall have a friend, and go to him at midnight and say to him, 'Friend, lend me three loaves; for a friend of mine has come to me on his journey, and I have nothing to set before him'; and he will answer from within and say, 'Do not trouble me; the door is now shut, and my children are with me in bed; I cannot rise and give to you'? I say to you, though he will not rise and give to him because he is his friend, yet because of his persistence he will rise and give him as many as he needs."
>
> —LUKE 11:5–8

He then encourages an ever-increasing level of passion in prayer: ask, seek, and knock!

> So I say to you, ask, and it will be given to you; seek, and you will find; knock, and it will be opened to you. For everyone who asks receives, and he who seeks finds, and to him who knocks it will be opened.
>
> —LUKE 11:9–10

He promises an open door to all who come to Him in prayer. Luke then gives the following encouragement:

> If you then, being evil, know how to give good gifts to your children, how much more will your heavenly Father give the Holy Spirit to those who ask Him!
>
> —LUKE 11:13

Righteous prayer results in the giving of the Holy Spirit and all His gifts and graces! Persistent and passionate prayers will lead to a release of the gift of the Holy Spirit. Could that include tongues?

Understanding the Great Commission

> Later He appeared to the eleven as they sat at the table; and He rebuked their unbelief and hardness of heart, because they did not believe those who had seen Him after He had risen. And He said to them, "Go into all the world and preach the gospel to every creature. He who believes and is baptized will be saved; but he who does not believe will be condemned. And these signs will follow those who believe: In My name they will cast out demons; they will speak with new tongues; they will take up serpents; and if they drink anything deadly, it will by no means hurt them; they will lay hands on the sick, and they will recover." So then, after the Lord had spoken to them, He was received up into heaven, and sat down at the right hand of God. And they went out and preached everywhere, the Lord working with them and confirming the word through the accompanying signs. Amen.
>
> —MARK 16:14–20

Mark is the Gospel written within fifteen to twenty years of the life of Jesus. Here it is clearly written that "speaking in tongues" is a sign that accompanies not simply apostles but also those who are people of faith.

This passage is often rejected because of the verses on serpents and poison. Those verses are not an endorsement of snake handling or drinking poison. They are simply God's promise of His protection and power and His commission if obeyed. Paul was protected from an inadvertent snakebite on the island of Malta.

It would be difficult to conclude that Jesus did or did not speak with tongues. It is clear that He taught intimate prayer and promised these gifts to His church.

CHAPTER FIVE
Speaking in Tongues and Church History

URING THE LAST several years a new word has entered church theology. This word is *cessationism*. This is the belief that the gifts of the Spirit, the working of miracles, and other signs ceased with the last apostle or at the close of the biblical canon (the sixty-six books of the Bible). As you can see, there are contradictions as to when this supposed cessation took place.

The Last Apostle

Cessationists teach that the church movement changed dramatically at the death of the last apostle. By this time the last book of the Bible was written and all the supernatural gifts, including tongues, ceased! The only problem with this is there is not a single shred of evidence in Scripture or history in support of this conclusion. In fact, to believe in cessationism is to lift a twentieth-century tradition above Holy Scripture.

The last apostle to die was John, about A.D. 110. It would be two more centuries before the church councils would settle on the sixty-six books that comprise our Bible.

Cessationists' theory is based upon the following assumptions:

1. Miracles happen only to validate doctrines.

2. Miracles happen only when God inspires Scripture.

3. Those who believe in present-day tongues and other gifts are elevating their experience above Scripture.

Only Three Periods of Miracles

D. John MacArthur—following in the footsteps of the Calvinist scholar the late B. B. Warfield—declared that there are only three seasons of miracles in Scripture.[1] According to this theory miracles happened only:

1. From Moses to Joshua, giving us the Pentateuch

2. From Elijah to Elisha, giving us the prophets

3. During the time of Christ and the apostles, giving us the New Testament

The problem with this view is that it is not supported by Scripture, church history, or the early church fathers. Furthermore, it is completely blown away by the strong biblical evidence to the contrary. Author Jack Deere has pointed to the miracles in Scripture outside these three periods.[2] For instance, before Moses you have the rapture of Enoch, Noah's ark, the destruction of Sodom and Gomorrah, and the miracle of Isaac's birth, just to name a few. The same could be said for all the so-called gaps. The plain truth is that God never changes! He can do mighty works at all times.

Some of these authors who believe in cessationism use intellectualism to combat Pentecostal experiences. The late B. B. Warfield in his book *Counterfeit Miracles* says that "right thinking people" should reject tongues and miracles.[3]

Intellectual arrogance says that those who speak in tongues are ignorant. They would do well to listen to Paul where he says:

> But the natural man does not receive the things of the Spirit of God, for they are foolishness to him; nor can he know them, because they are spiritually discerned.
> —1 Corinthians 2:14

Biblical Support for the Continuation of Tongues

There are many scriptures that support the continuation of tongues and other gifts, but let's focus on two: 1 Corinthians 1:4–8 and 1 Corinthians 13:8–13.

> I thank my God always concerning you for the grace of God which was given to you by Christ Jesus, that you were enriched in everything by Him in all utterance and all knowledge, even as the testimony of Christ was confirmed in you, so that you come short *in no gift*, eagerly waiting for the revelation of our Lord Jesus Christ, who will also confirm you to the end, that you may be blameless in the day of our Lord Jesus Christ.
> —1 Corinthians 1:4-8, emphasis added

In the original Greek, verse 7 indicates that the *charismata* (the supernatural gifts) will be operating at the coming of Jesus. Obviously they have not ceased! This is supported by another passage in the Corinthian letter.

> Love never fails. But whether there are prophecies, they will fail; whether there are tongues, they will cease; whether there is knowledge, it will vanish away. For we know in part and we prophesy in part. But when that which is perfect has come, then that which is in part will be done away. When I was a child, I spoke as a child, I understood as a child, I thought as a child; but when I became a man, I put away childish things. For now we see in a mirror, dimly, but then face to face. Now I know in part, but then I shall know just as I also am known. And now abide faith, hope, love these three; but the greatest of these is love.
> —I CORINTHIANS 13:8–13

These are the verses most misused by cessationists. They cite verses 8 and 10 to prove tongues have ceased. In verse 10 they interpret *perfect* to be the closing of the biblical canon. In other words, when the Bible was complete, tongues ceased. (See chapter 6.) Most New Testament scholars, however, support the interpretation that *perfect* represents the second coming of Christ.

History Speaks

Let us take a brief journey through the rest of church history to see if we find cessation or continuation of tongues.

Between 99 and 165 Justin Martyr ministered in the early church. In his *Dialogue With Trypho* he says, "Now it is possible to see amongst us women and men who possess gifts of the Spirit of God...."[4] Obviously Justin was ten years old when the last apostle died, so the gifts continued.

In a time span ranging from 130 to 202 Irenaeus cited in his book *Against Heresies* the operation of all the gifts, including tongues, exorcism, miracles, healings, and dead raised.[5]

Tertullian, who served a mega church in the third century, challenged the heretic Marcion to prove his validity by speaking in tongues.[6] How interesting! Here was a third-century church father waiting in expectation with a challenge that if one came preaching anything, he ought to be able to prove himself by the demonstration of tongues!

Dr. Montgomery's church history website reports accurately of similar instances of tongues by Urbanus; Nouatian; Hilary of Portieis (Catholic, 367); Ambrose (Catholic, 397); John Chrysostom, bishop of 10,000 in Constantinople (400); and St. Augustine (430).[7]

Obviously the gift of tongues continued after the apostles.

As we continue through church history we find no cessation of tongues even though the supernatural waned during dry seasons of spiritual coldness.

It is interesting to note that even John MacArthur admits, "...after the apostles tongues speaking was *almost* entirely in the Gnostics and Montanists."[8]

As I cite in my book *Awakened by the Spirit*, tongues, or what they called ecstatic expression, can be found among the fringes of Christianity all through history.[9]

A quick survey will find tongues among the following groups around the world until present day.

From 150 until 1000 such groups as the Montanists,

Novations, Donatists, Paulicians, and others spoke in tongues. (The Montanists were accused of being heretics, but so are Pentecostals today by some. See *Awakened by the Spirit* for a defense of Montanism.)

From 1100 to 1200 you had the Waldenses and the followers of Frances of Assisi all giving credence to tongues.

From 1300 to 1700 we find the gift of tongues among the Anabaptists, prophecy movement, Huguenots in France, Quakers in England, and later among the Pietists (Moravians) in Germany and Methodists in England and America.

From 1800 until the present we have ecstatic utterances evident in the second Great Awakening, Red River Revival, Holiness movement, Azusa and Pentecostal movement, healing revival under Smith Wigglesworth, A. A. Allen, Oral Roberts, and many others. Furthermore, tongues were very prominent in the charismatic movement and the Jesus movement in the 1960s and 1970s.

Speaking in tongues is happening in all major denominations across the world. Furthermore, the rise of charismatic magazines and books is a phenomenon. Also, Christian television is predominantly charismatic and has spread the message of spiritual gifts.

Clearly there is historical evidence for speaking in tongues. This is why, in spite of his caution, Paul warns the early church, "Do not forbid to speak with tongues" (1 Cor. 14:39).

CHAPTER SIX
Speaking in Tongues and the Church

L ET US AGAIN clearly understand speaking in tongues. Tongues is the spirit of man praying to God or speaking for God in a language the speaker has never learned (1 Cor. 14:2). Their language can be one of the six thousand–plus languages of men or a language of the spiritual realm (1 Cor. 13:1). This language is given by the Holy Spirit (Acts 2:4). Praying in tongues is not understood unless there is an interpretation given (1 Cor. 14:13-15). Tongues authenticated the mission of the believer (Mark 16:17).

Understanding this, it is important to observe a distinction between the prophetic tongues, which brings a revelation to the church, and a prayer experience, which is private (1 Cor. 14:5). Confusion can arise in the church if the private gift is exercised in the assembly without an interpretation. This does not exclude the use of uninterpreted tongues from all worship. In Acts 10:46 the church used tongues to magnify God. Also, Colossians 3:16 indicates singing in the Spirit, which could include singing in tongues. If carefully led and the church body is flowing together, tongues certainly can bring glory to God. The abrupt interruption of someone else's message, prayer, or song is confusing and wrong (1 Cor. 14:26-33).

In 1 Corinthians 14:14 Paul separates the public tongues from the private prayer language. Whereas the public tongue must be interpreted and the worship in tongues explained and practiced in harmony, the prayer language is private and serves a different purpose. (See next chapter.)

My First Experience With Tongues and Interpretation

After I was baptized in the Holy Spirit, I had several experiences that were the beginning of speaking in tongues. Finally, the dam broke, and I received a prayer language.

As I lay before the Lord one night, praying for a pastor friend who was facing life-changing career decisions, I sensed something rising in my spirit man. I felt wave after wave of joy in the presence of the Lord Jesus. The power of His presence soon issued praise from my lips. As I prayed aloud, other syllables, strange to my mind, began to come, and I continued to speak them forth.

At the end of that season of prayer, I asked the Lord for an interpretation. He quickened my mind with a word of warning for my friend not to take the staff position he had been offered. I immediately phoned him with the word.

Within seven days the pastor for whom he would have worked resigned. Had my friend gone into that position, he would have been left swinging in the breeze.

The biblical terms are nonthreatening in the Greek New Testament. *Glossa* means "tongues or language." *Laleo* means "to speak." Thus *glossolalia* means "to speak in tongues or languages." *Charismatic* comes from the Greek *charismata*, which means "grace gifts." Several wonderful English words are related to the Greek word *charis*: *grace, Messiah, anoint,* and *joy,* to name a few.

My mind then began to think of people across the years of my ministry. In every church along the way, I remembered that some of my finest and most faithful members had told me of their own gift of tongues. None of them fit the picture of divisive or arrogant. Not one ever told me I was not saved or spiritually inferior because I disagreed with their position. They smiled a lot, prayed a lot, gave a lot, and never questioned my leadership or teaching.

Problems never arose from those Spirit-filled people; rather, the problems always came when *other* members began to fear the freedom that those people had in Christ. I had looked down on those folks as if they were not quite as biblically smart as I was. Yet not once had any of those precious people done anything to upset the church. They practiced their gifts quietly.

For years I had thundered from the pulpit, "Tongues have ceased!" I based my position on 1 Corinthians 13:8. I had read all the standard cessationist interpretations. Now I was forced to look again at 1 Corinthians 13. It said, "Tongues will cease," in the future tense. This ceasing will happen when the "perfect" comes (v. 10). Although a few believe this "perfect" refers to the close of the biblical canon or completion of the written Scriptures, I discovered that most scholars interpret "perfect" as a reference to the second coming of Jesus. When He comes, the necessity for all the spiritual gifts will disappear.

Billy Graham has recently rereleased his book on the Holy Spirit. I was surprised to discover that Dr. Graham does not believe that tongues have ceased. He defines his view in this way:

> Although there is honest disagreement among Christians about the validity of tongues today, I personally cannot find any biblical justification for saying the gift of tongues was meant exclusively for New Testament times....Indeed, tongues is a gift of the Spirit....Today there are Presbyterians, Baptists, Anglicans, Lutherans, and Methodists, as well as Pentecostals, who speak or have spoken in tongues.[1]

Somehow it seems more comfortable for many Christians to believe that all of these spiritual manifestations have ceased than to worry about the modern church controlling the free expression of the gifts. Today we want an orderly church without the volatile and embarrassing disruptions brought on by an unleashed Holy Spirit. Listen to Michael Green:

> It is simply not the case that healing, prophecy, exorcism, and speaking in tongues died out with the last apostle. Still less can a passage like 1 Corinthians 13:8 ("as for prophecies, they will pass away; as for tongues, they will cease...") be used to attest the supposed demise of these gifts.[2]

You see, the gifts will pass away when the perfect comes at the Second Coming, not at the end of the apostolic age or after the formation of the New Testament canon, as some believe. There is plenty of evidence in the post-apostolic days and periodically throughout church history to show that these gifts did not die out in the first century.

First Corinthians 1:4–7 demonstrates that Paul expected all the gifts to be in operation at the end of the age:

> I thank my God always concerning you for the grace of God which was given to you by Christ Jesus, that you were enriched in every thing by Him in all utterance and all knowledge, even as the testimony of Christ was confirmed in you, so that you come short in no gift, eagerly waiting for the revelation of our Lord Jesus Christ.

Many scholars, such as Michael Green, Jack Deere, Michael Brown, and Wesley Campbell, cite the postapostolic material and historical references to an unbroken line of usage among some groups across the years. In chapter 5 we took a walk through history to see the evidence of the Holy Spirit through the ages.

The Use of Prophetic Tongues Today

The subject of tongues continues to cause debate among Christian scholars, but I believe that the Bible teaches that there are varied giftings of tongues. One of these is a prayer language available to *every* Christian for individual edification, and another is a prophetic gift of tongues given to edify the church body.

The prophetic gift of tongues is often misused and misunderstood. Paul addressed the Corinthian Christians on this issue, for he was concerned that they esteemed the gift so highly that it threatened to overcome the other aspects of worship.

First Corinthians 14 records some strong cautions and careful guidelines for its use in public worship. In the gathered public church, the gift of tongues should be a rare occurrence. Paul limited its use to *three* times in a gathering and required that each speak separately. The guidelines further indicate an interpreter is required. If someone pronounces a message in a tongue during a service and no interpretation comes, the person should be commanded to keep silent.

The benefits of tongues when interpreted in a service can be great. The prophetic message can build up, encourage, and comfort others in the church, providing words of vision and expectation.

We must be aware that demons can counterfeit tongues. Just as people can be influenced by demons to make false professions of faith, so can Satan transform himself as a minister of unrighteousness.

Avoiding tongues because of misuse is not necessary, however. We would never consider giving up preaching because some people responding to the sermons made phony decisions.

The simple answer to this caution is to obey 1 John 4:1–2 and test the spirit by asking the person to privately pray in tongues in the presence of a mature believer. The counselor can ask the spirit praying in tongues to confess Jesus as Lord in English. I have seen the gift of tongues verified many times in this manner.

On some occasions, though, I have heard the demonic

imitation. While I was preaching in another city, I was distracted during an altar call by a woman who was crying out loudly, bending over. I sensed it was a disruption, so I proceeded to test the spirit. She responded to the test by crying, "Jesus is *a* lord." I replied, "Is He your Lord?" The demon in her answered me, screaming, "No, He is not my Lord." Subsequently we cast the demon out of the woman and led her to Christ. She was a leader and a worker in her church, and yet she had a false tongue.

Beware of the counterfeit gifts given by demons. Satan counterfeits only what is valuable. Human counterfeiters aren't interested in counterfeiting pennies. They counterfeit valuable currency. Likewise, demons want people to receive a phony substitute for the true power of God.

A second caution is to avoid spiritual pride. Though many godly men claim so, a person does not have to have the gift of tongues as an evidence of the power and anointing of the Holy Spirit. Don't try to force your gift on others, and humble yourself in the hands of God who gives gifts as He chooses.

As stated earlier, caution must be used when tongues are exercised in a public worship service. The guidelines given in 1 Corinthians 14 should be followed, and an interpretation should always occur. The pastor or leader should exercise discretion because demonic imitation of prophetic words could cause spiritual confusion in the church.

The habit of many well-meaning believers of coming up behind inquirers during an altar call and praying in tongues can be distracting. It could distract the unsaved from hearing the gospel. Your prayer language should not be exercised in the presence of the uninformed, so that you do not cause confusion or division.

It is the task of the pastor to preach and teach the church. It is never appropriate to interrupt the teaching and preaching of God's Word by an individual speaking either in tongues or in a natural language.

Primarily because of the misuse and abuse of tongues, division and misunderstanding have arisen over the years. A believer with this gift should be careful of the context in which he exercises the gift. Using this gift around people who are unfamiliar with and uninformed of its use would not be loving or appropriate.

After saying all this, I must carefully state that I would not presume to limit God's working, but I caution you as a believer to be sensitive to the Holy Spirit.

Those who speak in tongues are not better than those who don't. Don't criticize the gift or be jealous of those who have it. Be grateful for all the gifts in the body of Christ. One of the greatest blessings in the Christian life is the diversity of gifts in believers. As God's power rests on each of His children, the body reaps the benefits.

The church today has no need to chase after signs such as tongues. Jesus promised that these and other signs would follow as believers' hearts grow hungry (Mark 16). We must be balanced, not bigoted, toward tongues. Remember, saving lost souls is our goal.

CHAPTER SEVEN
Speaking in Tongues and the Individual

Ａs I STATED in the last chapter, the New Testament differentiates between the public use of tongues and the private prayer experience. But what good is a prayer language? Is tongues pure emotional babble? Are there blessings that come from speaking in tongues?

The benefits of tongues when interpreted in a service can be great. The prophetic message can build up, encourage, and comfort others in the church, providing words of vision and expectation.

Though the prophetic gift of tongues may be of limited use in public worship today, its use for the individual believer is clearly taught in Scripture. In spite of all the precautions cited in 1 Corinthians 14 having to do with the practice of tongues, Paul strongly warned the enemies of freedom, "Do not forbid to speak with tongues" (1 Cor. 14:39). And he declared, "I speak with tongues more than you all" (v. 18).

In Gordon Fee's monumental work *God's Empowering Presence: The Holy Spirit in the Letters of Paul*, he says this:

> I was overwhelmed as I realized the depth of Paul's reliance on the supernatural work and power of the Holy Spirit. Paul prayed and sang in the Spirit. The legalistic Pharisee who seemed so stern broke out in

joy and freedom at his conversion. Even in describing the kingdom of God, Paul could hardly contain himself as he shouted, "The kingdom of God is not eating and drinking, but righteousness and peace and joy in the Holy Spirit."[1]

The Benefits of a Private Prayer Language

Even those who concede the possibility of the continuation of the gifts often find tongues an insurmountable roadblock. Further, those who are willing to accept the public, congregational use of tongues are stymied by the idea of a "private prayer language." "It makes no sense," they argue. "Tongues edifies the body [of the church], but the believer can't even understand what they're babbling in private." What then are the benefits of this unique gift from God? Rest assured, they are many!

Releases a joyful new connection to God

The first benefit we see in tongues is that the gift releases joy in the believer's life. The gift of tongues allows one's spirit to communicate directly to God's Spirit: "For he who speaks in a tongue does not speak to men but to God" (1 Cor. 14:2). This closeness of fellowship releases joy.

Many times when tongues are mentioned, we find that individuals also "magnify God," such as in Acts 10:46. When Mary exalted God in expectation of the birth of Jesus, she declared, "My spirit has rejoiced in God my Savior" (Luke 1:47). The translation in Greek for this word literally means "jump for joy." Although we don't know that Mary praised God in tongues, there was a literal move in her spirit in response to the joy of the Holy Spirit, who had overshadowed her in preparation for the coming of Jesus.

In our Western Christianity, we seem to be saturated by an approach to God based on Greek philosophy and rationalism rather than the power of the Holy Spirit. I am not anti-intellectual and do not believe anyone should put his brain on the shelf when he comes to church. After all, we are told to love the Lord our God with all our heart, soul, and *mind*! However, our minds are darkened and corrupt, and we are ever battling the natural man, or the flesh. Clearly, we are told, "The natural man does not receive the things of the Spirit of God" (1 Cor. 2:14). In other words, our flesh fights things that are not explainable.

A spiritual realm exists whereby God communicates to the spirit and then to the mind. Only as we offer ourselves in brokenness and surrender can God renew our minds and reveal Himself to us.

Releases spiritual understanding

Speaking in tongues may bring the capacity to understand some of life's mysteries: "In the spirit he speaks mysteries" (1 Cor. 14:2). We often do not know how to pray as we ought, but through the Spirit the way is revealed. In fact, we learn that the Spirit Himself prays for us, as revealed in Romans 8:26–27:

> Likewise the Spirit also helps in our weaknesses. For we do not know what we should pray for as we ought, but the Spirit Himself makes intercession for us with groanings which cannot be uttered. Now He who searches the hearts knows what the mind of the

Spirit is, because He makes intercession for the saints according to the will of God.

The Holy Spirit prays for us when we do not know how. The Father knows our needs before we ask. I am convinced a person can be led of the Spirit to pray in his native language; however, God has also provided a language of prayer by which we may communicate spirit to Spirit with the Lord. Paul addressed this at length in 1 Corinthians 14:

> For he who speaks in a tongue does not speak to men but to God, for no one understands him; however, in the spirit he speaks mysteries....He who speaks in a tongue edifies himself, but he who prophesies edifies the church....For if I pray in a tongue, my spirit prays, but my understanding is unfruitful. What is the conclusion then? I will pray with the spirit, and I will also pray with the understanding. I will sing with the spirit, and I will also sing with the understanding.
> —1 Corinthians 14:2, 4, 14–15

Paul spent most of 1 Corinthians 14 addressing the need for interpretation to accompany tongues in public worship. However, he reminded the believers that there are great benefits to using tongues in private prayer. He encouraged them to use their gifts properly.

There is a mystery about prayer, which causes us to ask why we need to pray if God is ever present and all-knowing. The answer is this: we pray not to inform God but to adjust our lives to what He has already set in motion. It pleases God for us to pray. He has called us to intercession. He willed to operate only in answer to prayer. A person may pray with the

Spirit or with the understanding. As we pray in the Spirit, God moves through us to pray for what our flesh could never comprehend.

In 1 Corinthians 4:1 we discover that we are "stewards of the mysteries of God." "Steward" could also be translated "manager." As a manager, one must know how to get and transfer resources where they may be needed.

A hidden wisdom predates the creative order. This wisdom was not some higher human knowledge revealed only to a select few, as some believe. It was a revelation of God's purpose revealed by the Spirit to the praying Christian.

As we open up the spirit man to God, the Scriptures become more alive to us. The power of God is released. The Holy Spirit quickens the spirit and anoints us to receive the truth from God's Word. Instead of our learning Scripture as history or literature, the Holy Spirit gives us the capacity to grasp the "things of God" as we read the inspired Word of God. An anointing of understanding comes upon believers.

> But the anointing which you have received from Him abides in you, and you do not need that anyone teach you; but as the same anointing teaches you concerning all things, and is true, and is not a lie, and just as it has taught you, you will abide in Him.
> —1 JOHN 2:27

Paul had a working knowledge of the Old Testament before he was saved and filled with the Spirit. However, as Paul prayed in the Spirit and experienced the very presence of God, the Holy Spirit gave him a deeper understanding of the Scriptures. It is the same today; the Holy Spirit does not bring new truth but brings new revelation of the truth already revealed in Scripture as we pray in the Spirit. We are heart to heart with God without the filter of our flesh.

This special revelation will cause you to stop in the middle of your reading of a Scripture passage and feel as though a verse is leaping off the page in bold clarity. The verse may seem to come alive to you and speak to you personally and directly.

Releases power and strength

Prayer in the Spirit will strengthen the inner man. While the Holy Spirit freely uses a number of ways to encourage and fortify believers, a prayer language is one means He uses to strengthen us. The primary use of tongues today is for personal edification, or the building up of the individual's spirit for ministry.

First Corinthians 14:4 is often cited critically to condemn tongues as a selfish gift: "He who speaks in a tongue edifies himself." It is true that gifts are given to edify or build up the whole church as the body of Christ. However, the body is made up of individual members who need individual strength and blessing. In this verse Paul told of the benefits of his prayer language and, as we already read in verse 15 of the same chapter, again emphasized his determination to continue the practice in his own life when he stated, "I will pray with the spirit, and I will also pray with the understanding." He knew that the corporate body is only as strong as its individual members and that he must privately continue to exercise a gift that God specifically gave him to strengthen him in ministry.

If I play on a football team, would I be considered selfish for taking part in personal training in order to build up my strength? Would I be selfish because I exercised and lifted weights? Of course not, for my individual strength would be added to the team's strengths. A prayer language can strengthen the inner man. Paul prayed for his fellow believers to learn this truth so that they may "be strengthened with might through His Spirit in the inner man" (Eph. 3:16). This strengthening includes a confirmation of the faith, what we believe, as well as the ability to exercise faith in the work of God. Read the twentieth and twenty-first verses of Jude:

> But you, beloved, building yourselves up on your most
> holy faith, praying in the Holy Spirit, keep yourselves
> in the love of God, looking for the mercy of our Lord
> Jesus Christ unto eternal life.

Because the believer is built up through prayer in the Holy Spirit, there is an enablement to "keep [oneself] in the love of God" and also to "look for the mercy of our Lord Jesus Christ." Beyond that, this "building up" includes releasing the ability to publicly prophesy or proclaim the Word of God. The gift of tongues stirs up the prophetic gift. In 1 Corinthians 14:5 the text reveals, "I wish you all spoke with tongues, but even more that you prophesied." Listen to that phrase, "but even more that you prophesied." The English translations don't communicate the full effect of the original Greek. If you investigate this verse word for word in any of the excellent concordances or interlinear Greek texts, you'll find that this is the more literal translation: "I would that you spoke with tongues much in order that you may prophesy greater."

Paul would also say that five understood words are better than ten thousand in tongues when those tongues cannot be clearly interpreted. We should also consider that a person ought to pray ten thousand words privately in his closet before he speaks before the people of God. As I go early to my office on Sunday morning before I step out to preach to the church body, I find I must spend time exercising my prayer language. It is in no way a mere ritual; rather, it builds up my spirit and stimulates the prophetic gift in me so that I can speak His Word with boldness.

Releases a new dimension of worship

Tongues can also be a form of worship for the believer. Paul confessed to singing in the Spirit as well as praying in the Spirit. In Acts 10:46 it is recorded that "they heard them speak with tongues and magnify God." On the Day of Pentecost, both a miracle of speaking and a miracle of understanding occurred. The apostles spoke in ecstatic utterance, and many dialects were understood.

If you picture the scene at Pentecost, you would have to admit this occurrence likely did not include prophetic, interpreted tongues. Thousands of people had gathered to investigate what had happened to the apostles. A mighty wind was howling through the room at the same time that all the loud voices of the apostles were praising God in tongues. Yet above all the noise, people heard in their own languages the tongues at Pentecost giving praise to God!

This incident seems to involve a miracle of hearing as well

as understanding because no interpreter is mentioned in the Book of Acts. Tongues were useful for worship and praise in the presence of believers. Though I don't wish to say God cannot work as He chooses, I feel Scripture indicates that for the most part, when tongues are used in public worship, an interpreter is required.

Releasing the Gifts of Tongues

A study of Scripture reveals that speaking in tongues was likely the most common gift practiced by believers in the early church. It was definitely the first sign of gifts released in the early church. How can you recognize and release this gift in your own life? There is a process:

1. You will have a desire for intimacy with the Lord.

2. You will sense your spirit man and the Spirit of God desiring to communicate.

3. The Holy Spirit will rise within you, and your spirit man will speak through vocal cords.

4. You must exercise your will. You must choose to speak by opening your mouth and allowing the language of heaven to pour forth.

5. Your spirit will know this language, and you will be able to speak this language at will. Furthermore, you can stop speaking at will.

If you don't receive this gift, do not fret or feel inferior. God may desire to release other gifts in you. Later, God may give you this gift as well.

CHAPTER EIGHT
Speaking in Tongues as Evidence of Spirit Baptism

ENTECOSTALISM IS CONSIDERED by many to be a faulty new phenomenon in church history. I would dispute that based on the fact that apostolic, Pentecostal Christianity has an unbroken line in the history of the church, as I have briefly demonstrated in the chapter on church history and tongues.

As a fast growing, mainstream movement, Pentecostalism has now come to the forefront. The rising of Pentecostalism and speaking in tongues has certain markers. The Holiness movement of the nineteenth century gave birth to modern-day Pentecostalism.

I have discovered books such as Asa Mahan's *The Baptism of the Holy Ghost*, written in 1870, and William Arthur's *The Tongue of Fire*, which was written between 1856 and 1870. Though I do not have copies, the titles seem to predict what was coming. Rev. Charles Parham, a Holiness preacher and president of Bethel Bible College, preached a revival in Topeka, Kansas. At the meeting a woman named Agnes Ozmar spoke in tongues. She was a Methodist!

Coming out of that school and revival was an African American preacher named William Seymour. He started a church in Los Angeles, California. That meeting was attended by both Anglo-Americans and African Americans. They came from the Baptist church and the Holiness church. Some came from First Baptist Church Los Angeles, where under Rev. Joseph Smale fourteen weeks of revival had broken out, only to be rejected by the deacons.[1]

On April 9, 1906, a man named Edward Lee and a woman named Jennie Moore spoke in tongues. The Azusa Street Apostolic Faith Mission was born. This movement spread from there until it swept around the world. Early on it was primarily Holiness churches that became Pentecostal Holiness churches. Other groups sprung up that are now large movements, such as the Church of God in Christ, Church of God (Cleveland, TN), the Assemblies of God, and others. This powerful movement has broken down racial, gender, and denominational walls.

Three Main Groups of Pentecostals

First, some with Holiness background believed that believers must be justified (saved), fully sanctified (new life from the Spirit), and baptized by the Holy Spirit with tongues as the initial evidence. Let me quickly say that most Pentecostal associations no longer embrace this three-step process.

Second, you have other Pentecostals such as the Assemblies of God who do not include the second step of total sanctification but believe any Christian can be baptized by the Holy Spirit. They believe that tongues is the initial evidence of this baptism.

Third, you have the Oneness or "Jesus only" who believe that the early church water baptism was done in the name of

Jesus Christ only. This group also believes that tongues is the initial evidence of the baptism of the Holy Spirit.

Support for Evidential Tongues

I found two strong supports for evidential tongues. First, the biblical account in the Book of Acts. When we begin to trace the historical record of Dr. Luke, we find strong support for speaking in tongues as an evidence for the baptism with the Spirit. Let us look at the record in Acts 2:2–4:

> And suddenly there came a sound from heaven, as of a rushing mighty wind, and it filled the whole house where they were sitting. Then there appeared to them divided tongues, as of fire, and one sat upon each of them. And they were all filled with the Holy Spirit and began to speak with other tongues, as the Spirit gave them utterance.

You have at the Day of Pentecost the baptism of the Holy Spirit prophesied by John the Baptist and promised by Jesus. (See Luke 3:16; 24:49; Acts 1:5.)

Clearly on the Day of Pentecost there was a miracle of speaking in tongues and a miracle of understanding. As you journey on through the Book of Acts, you have what has been called the Gentile Pentecost in Acts 10:44–48:

> While Peter was still speaking these words, the Holy Spirit fell upon all those who heard the word. And those of the circumcision who believed were astonished…because the gift of the Holy Spirit had been poured out on the Gentiles also. For they heard them speak with tongues and magnify God. Then

> Peter answered, "Can anyone forbid water, that these should not be baptized who have received the Holy Spirit just as we have?" And he commanded them to be baptized in the name of the Lord. Then they asked him to stay a few days.

Here the Holy Spirit falls on the house of Cornelius, and again they speak in tongues. Later Peter would use the outpouring at the house of Cornelius and speaking in tongues as evidence that Gentiles could be included in the family.

Thirteen years later at Ephesus God fell again with the same manifestation of speaking in tongues (Acts 19:1–7).

As a side note, it is interesting that in Revelation 2 Jesus calls the church at Ephesus to return to its first love and first works. Obviously, the first works included speaking in tongues as an evidence for Spirit baptism. It seems that the biblical record indicates a releasing of tongues when people are baptized in the Spirit.

A second proof, I believe, is found in the problems with tongues in Corinth. Tongues was clearly the most prevalent gift, and since so many had at least a prayer language, misuse had arisen. Since the prayer language was common, it could be a problem.

Beyond these two proofs let me suggest as well that the baptism with the Holy Spirit is called "a pledge" or "a guarantee" of the inheritance in the world to come (Eph. 1:14). (See my book *An Essential Guide to Baptism in the Holy Spirit*.)

This "seal," or "guarantee," was an outward visible manifestation of God's work in someone's life. Could tongues be evidence of that pledge?

Finally, as I have demonstrated, there seems to be an outbreak of speaking in tongues, ecstatic experience, and unusual works at outbreaks of awakening.

An Evidence or *the* Evidence?

Here is where the controversy rages among Pentecostals and charismatics. I think at this point we must use love as our guide. In 1 Corinthians 13:1 Paul says that "tongues" are no more than a noise if we do not demonstrate agape love. We must understand that "speaking in tongues" cannot be found as an essential part of any apostolic creed or confession from the early church. As important as this gift is to believers, it was *never* a test of fellowship.

Let me say further that there is no clear statement to the affect that speaking in tongues is the evidence for Spirit baptism in the New Testament. Our belief in tongues must not be equated with Christ's virgin birth, the Trinity, the cross, the resurrection, and the second coming of Christ.

While I do believe that everyone can have a prayer language, I know some who have had transforming experiences with the Holy Spirit and yet not had this release. Others I have known have had such an experience but feel it is a private love language between them and God.

Furthermore, the elevation of speaking in tongues and its abuse have driven people away from the saving message of Jesus Christ. Even Paul had to harness the misuse of tongues at the church in Corinth.

Abba Father and Spirit Baptism

More evidence and a simple beginning point for those who receive the baptism with the Holy Spirit may be found in two New Testament scriptures. Listen to Paul in Galatians 4:4–7 as he describes God sending the Holy Spirit into one's life:

> But when the fullness of the time had come, God sent forth His Son, born of a woman, born under the law, to redeem those who were under the law, that we might receive the adoption as sons. And because you are sons, God has sent forth the Spirit of His Son into your hearts, crying out, "Abba, Father!" Therefore you are no longer a slave but a son, and if a son, then an heir of God through Christ.

Paul describes Christ's saving work to rescue believers from the death decreed by the law. As a result of this a second realization of blessing comes. God sends His Spirit into our hearts "crying out 'Abba, Father.'"

An initial work of the Holy Spirit is the believer being marked off as a son or heir of Abba Father. *Abba* is the Hebrew and Arabic term of affection for one's father, like one's English Daddy or Papa!

Paul then records the believers' response to this entrance of the Holy Spirit crying "Abba, Father" in the eighth chapter, verses 12–16, of his letter to the Romans:

> Therefore, brethren, we are debtors—not to the flesh, to live according to the flesh. For if you live according to the flesh, you will die; but if by the Spirit you put to

> death the deeds of the body, you will live. For as many
> as are led by the Spirit of God, these are sons of God.
> For you did not received the spirit of bondage again to
> fear, but you received the Spirit of adoption by whom
> we cry out, "Abba, Father." The Spirit Himself bears
> witness with our spirit that we are children of God.

When we are freshly baptized by the Holy Spirit, "we cry out, 'Abba, Father.'" Now we are no longer limited by the flesh, captive to our old desires, nor are we without direction or a future. Even suffering can be understood because the Holy Spirit has marked us as children of Abba Father. I believe that we embrace the full work of the Holy Spirit by confessing Him to be our Abba Father on Earth today. Yet, after that we can experience a deeper level of intimacy that could and should include speaking in tongues.

CHAPTER NINE

Speaking in Tongues and Science

Years ago during the 1970s charismatic movement a report got out that a study was made at a university in Toronto, Canada, that refuted tongues. The report stated that the language department had tape-recorded tongues and could find no evidence of any language. When I began to search for this study, I could find no record of it! My research found that the so-called study at Toronto was a research paper done by a graduate student. A phone call to the University of Toronto resulted in their denial of any such study! Yet this story continues to circulate thirty years later.

In fact, new languages and dialects are still very common in the world. When I was a student at Samford University, my Greek professor suggested that there are over six thousand known languages in our world! How could anyone possibly be able to decide what is and what is not a language? Beyond that, Paul speaks of "tongues of angels." This indicates that there are more languages available from the heavenly dimensions.

New York Times and Tongues

In 2006 Benedict Carey wrote an account of research done at the University of Pennsylvania on speaking in tongues.

This article is widely available and on the *New York Times* website.

In this article they speak of "the passionate, sometimes rhythmic language-like pattern that pours forth from those who speak in tongues."[1] In research at the university they took brain images of five women as they were speaking in tongues and "found that their frontal lobes—the thinking, willful part of the brain through which people control what they do—were relatively quiet, as were the language centers." These images have been shown in *Psychiatry Research: Neuroimaging* and show that the images support people's interpretation of what was happening.[2]

The study team included Dr. Andrew Newberg, Donna Morgan, Nancy Wintering, and Mark Waldman. Since the human language center of the brain is quiet, then it seems God is talking through them. Science supports the fact that genuine tongues comes from outside the believer. They further report that the person receives positive affects, pleasure, and positive emotions.[3]

Science affirms that tongues comes from outside the mind of the believer! All of a sudden we find that the believer who speaks in tongues is communicating on a level that science understands but cannot explain.

Mozart and Tongues

There is a best-selling book called *The Mozart Effect* by Don Campbell that talks about the power of music to heal.[4] Now, the book is not a Christian book, and I do not agree with all the author's conclusions; however, the book contains some interesting truths. One, the music composed by Mozart at age six has healing power. Mozart believed that music came from God. Notable miracles have happened when children are exposed to the classical music of Christian composers. There are remarkable stories of healing to be found in this book. Interestingly, Campbell had students repeat phrases that they did not understand over and over again. He calls this practice "secular glossolalia." Though not clear, I believe Campbell has drawn this sound from genuine tongues speaking. The students who speak in tongues feel remarkably refreshed by the experience.[5] I do not recommend this; I am simply reporting the credibility for tongues given by scientific research.

Campbell also cites the remarkable healing power of the Gregorian chant, a form of Christian praise and worship, from long ago. The Benedictine monasteries have restored this ancient music. This method of plainsong, as it was called, was introduced by Pope Gregory the Great at the end of the sixth century. The chant was received as a dove flying in representing the Holy Spirit.[6] Pope Gregory said that the Holy Spirit whispered the chant into his ear and his spirit sang it.[7]

This powerful music from heaven seems to be like singing in tongues. It was revived in the twentieth century and has given new life to the spirit of man.[8] The Gregorian chant, according to Campbell, "allowed practitioners to prepare for this journey by living in two worlds at once."[9] Today the Benedictines believe the heavenly choir of angels joins their chants and blesses them with a never-ending cycle of sonic inspiration.[10]

Paul spoke of singing in tongues in 1 Corinthians 14:15. In the late 1940s and early 1950s there was a movement called the heavenly choir. At this present time while praising the Lord, our church will often move into a God-guided rhythm of music and tongues not learned or on the written program.

Worship Strengthened

Tongues can be used prophetically to edify the church. Tongues can be used prayerfully to strengthen the individual. Tongues can also be released musically. This heavenly rhythm glorifies God and brings the heavenly dimension to earth. When this happens and heaven opens, then unusual miracles and healings may occur. Our fallen bodies can experience the eternal rhythm of the heavenlies. In such a state our souls can be restored.

In Acts 10:45–46, Luke records a significant moment in the history of the universal church:

> And those of the circumcision who believed were astonished, as many as came with Peter, because the gift of the Holy Spirit had been poured out on the Gentiles also. For they heard them speak with tongues and magnify God.

Peter and other Jews had come to Caesarea from Joppa at the invitation of an Italian centurion named Cornelius. A *Gentile*! But God had given a very specific vision to Cornelius. In this vision God told him to send for Peter. While Cornelius's servants were on their way, Peter had his well-known rooftop vision. Here God prepared his heart to spread the word to the house of Cornelius.

This is where the story gets amazing. Peter agreed to go with the aforementioned group. When they arrived and preached the gospel to Cornelius and his household, we are told in Acts 10:44 that the "Holy Spirit fell upon all those who heard the word."

Now we have to revisit Acts 10:1–2. Here we see that Cornelius, a man who is described earlier in the chapter as a "devout man" who "feared God" and "gave alms generously to the people" but not one who had even heard of Jesus Christ, hears the gospel from the mouth of Peter. While he is hearing it, he begins speaking in tongues, along with all those present.

It was then that the Jews present were "astonished...because *the gift* of the Holy Spirit had been poured out on the Gentiles." Here tongues were not interpreted as prophecy or used as a prayer. In Acts 10:45 tongues came forth as a form of worship. God is magnified. He gets larger and we are smaller as His kingdom moves to the earth. Church then embraces the agenda of our Lord Jesus Christ.

So both science and Scripture welcome speaking in tongues.

CHAPTER TEN
Speaking in Tongues and Order

ONCE HEARD A dear brother in Christ say the great gifts of the Holy Spirit brought unity. There are many who believe this, but it is sadly not the case. We're told in Acts 2:1 that prior to the coming of the Holy Spirit:

> And when the Day of Pentecost had fully come, they were all with one accord in one place.

We see here that the unity was present before the Holy Spirit came. Regrettably, there has been unity and disunity in various times since Pentecost.

The Corinthian church had a serious problem with tongues.

What Speaking in Tongues Does Not Do

The Corinthian church was replete with divisions. Tongues did not stop division and disunity! Read 1 Corinthians 1:10–11 for the record:

> Now I plead with you, brethren, by the name of our Lord Jesus Christ, that you all speak the same thing, and that there be no divisions among you, but that you be perfectly joined together in the same mind and in the same judgment. For it has been declared to

> me concerning you, my brethren, by those of Chloe's
> household, that there are contentions among you.

Secondly, the Corinthians minimized the power of the cross while problems were magnified. Look at verses 11–17:

> For it has been declared to me concerning you, my
> brothers, by those of Chloe, that there are contentions
> among you. Now I say this, that each of you says, "I am
> of Paul," or "I am of Apollos," or " I am of Cephas," or
> "I am of Christ." Is Christ divided? Was Paul crucified
> for you? Or were you baptized in the name of Paul? I
> thank God that I baptized none of you except Crispus
> and Gaius, lest anyone should say that I had baptized
> in my own name. Yes, I also baptized the household of
> Stephanas. Besides, I do not know whether I baptized
> any other. For Christ did not send me to baptize, but
> to preach the gospel, not with wisdom of words, lest
> the cross of Christ should be made of no effect.

Imagine it! The Corinthians were so concerned over who had been baptized by whom (in modern-day parlance think, "What church are you a part of?" or "How many times has the pastor asked *you* to lunch?") that Paul said that they were, essentially, rendering the power of the cross void!

Third, a carnal immaturity dominated the church. We read in 1 Corinthians 3:1–3 that speaking in tongues did not alleviate this childishness:

> And I, brethren, could not speak to you as to spiritual
> people but as to carnal, as to babes in Christ. I fed
> you with milk and not with solid food; for until now
> you were not able to receive it, and even now you are

> still not able; for you are still carnal. For where there are envy, strife, and divisions among you, are you not carnal and behaving like mere men?

Here is evidence of believers filled with the Holy Spirit evidenced by speaking in other tongues, and yet so immature were they in their faith that Paul said he still had to feed them milk! These were Spirit-filled believers who were still carnal and lived like "like mere men."

Fourthly, and most shockingly, we read in 1 Corinthians 5:1 that speaking in tongues did not stop immorality of the worst kind.

> It is actually reported that there is sexual immorality among you, and such sexual immorality as is not even named among the Gentiles—that a man has his father's wife!

Let's look at this verse in segments.

It is actually reported . . .

Word of the sexual immorality and lifestyle choices made by the Corinthians had spread. It wasn't as if these were isolated incidents or that this behavior was coming from just one or two members in the church.

. . . that there is sexual immorality among you . . .

It was widely known that these Corinthian Christians were sexually immoral. Think on that! This church was best known for two things: speaking in tongues and sexual immorality. Take note here as well that the news of sins committed by professed Christians are quick to be spread by unbelievers.

... and such sexual immorality as is not
even named among the Gentiles ...

The act committed by at least one of the Corinthian believers was so horrific it was not even discussed as an option among the "heathen." A man had, at the very least, slept with his father's wife. The church at Corinth, full of "Spirit-filled, tongues-talkin', devil-stompin'" (as the saying goes) believers, not only accepted this man into fellowship but also apparently never rebuked him for his actions. Why is that? It's because speaking in tongues does not thwart immorality. We'll come back to this, but for now, let's continue.

Fifthly, speaking in tongues did not bring humility. Listen to the words Paul uses in 1 Corinthians 5:2 to rebuke that church:

> And you are puffed up, and have not rather mourned, that he who has done this deed might be taken away from among you.

As a result of the sexual immorality permitted and, by implication, endorsed by the Corinthian church, Paul told them that they should have mourned over this situation. Instead they were full of pride because they spoke in tongues and were filled with the Holy Spirit. How often do we see that today? Fellow believers and even church leaders have blindly turned their eyes away from sin; some have even used their Holy Spirit–enabled calling as a means to build a smokescreen over their sin. It is nothing more than the old problem of "Corinthian pride."

Sixth, speaking in tongues did not stop these believers from suing each other. Imagine it! But when you look around the universal church (evangelical, fundamentalist, and charismatic all have representation here), you don't have to imagine it because we're still doing it today. Listen to how Paul chastises them in 1 Corinthians 6:1–2 for their litigious nature.

> Dare any of you, having a matter against another, go to law before the unrighteous, and not before the saints? Do you not know that the saints shall judge the world? And if the world will be judged by you, are you unworthy to judge the smallest matters?

Don't misunderstand this. Paul is not saying that legal recourse is bad. What he is chastising here is the propensity on the part of the Corinthian believers to engage in vexatious lawsuits *with other church members*! He rebukes them and encourages them to follow what is, at its heart, a "Matthew 18" approach for matters such as these.

I believe there is good cause for this. Remember how quickly and widespread was the word of sexual immorality of the Corinthians among the "Gentiles" (the better term here is, "all the unsaved people")? The same idea applies here. Just as the Corinthians in their vice and permissiveness were disparaging the cross, so does this kind of trivial, immature, and self-serving behavior. We must take great care that the power of the cross is not made, through our own questionable behavior, of no effect.

Seventh, speaking in tongues did not promote healthy marriages in the Corinthian church. The young man mentioned in chapter 5 aside, the Corinthians had their fair share of marital issues. This is a thorny issue to be sure, but one we

must cover. Let's look first at what Paul says in 1 Corinthians
7:10–12 to the Corinthians:

> Now to the married I command, yet not I but the
> Lord: A wife is not to depart from her husband. But
> even if she does depart, let her remain unmarried or
> be reconciled to her husband. And a husband is not to
> divorce his wife. But to the rest I, not the Lord, say: If
> any brother has a wife who does not believe, and she is
> willing to live with him, let him not divorce her.

There is a large plot of ground to cover in these few verses,
and most of it is riddled with land mines, so let's tread
carefully.

In verse 10, Paul gives a command from the Lord that
addresses various sets of circumstances that the Corinthians
had written asking him. First, should spouses separate? The
apostle responds with the Lord's command: no. However, he
says, if it has already happened, let them remain unmarried
or, in hope of the best outcome, let them reconcile to each
other. The other issue at hand here was the scenario wherein
a believer found himself (or, I think, herself) married to an
unbeliever. Here Paul says plainly that this is not an issue
that should cause undue stress. Simply put, if the unbeliever
is content to stay married to the believer, then the believer
should stay married.

The point here is simply to say that the level and variance
of questions the apostle was called to address indicate mul-
tiple states of disorder in the marital lives of the believers in
Corinth.

Eighth, speaking in tongues did not guarantee doctrinal

soundness. This is a platform from which cessationists love to launch their offensive. Even today, there are many in the church who operate in miracles, tongues, and prophecies, but their doctrine is often not sound. The logical conclusion, opponents say, is that all of the signs are *ipso facto*, just as unsound. But let's look at the issues in 1 Corinthians 15:12 that Paul had to deal with in Corinth:

> Now if Christ is preached that He has been raised from the dead, how do some among you say that there is no resurrection of the dead?

The Corinthians, at least some of them, were denying one of the most basic doctrines of the faith. This, some might say, is not really an issue; "after all, if you believe in Jesus, that's really what saves you." But Paul addressed this attitude in the very next verses (vv. 13–14):

> But if there is no resurrection of the dead, then Christ is not risen. And if Christ is not risen, then our preaching is empty and *your faith is also empty*.
>
> —EMPHASIS ADDED

Yet, in all of this, the miracle of speaking in tongues was present in that church.

Ninth, speaking in tongues did not increase giving and promote church prosperity. If you listen to a lot of preachers and teachers today, you might be inclined to think that it actually goes the other way around, but as that is a subject for another time, let's stick to the issue with which Paul was confronted.

Christians in Judea were, at this time, greatly troubled

and persecuted, and it was the manner of various Gentile churches to take up special collections and send them to help their Judean brothers and sisters. However, in Corinth (and in Galatia) Paul had to give special instruction for them to take part in this. Read 1 Corinthians 16:1–2 and see.

> Now concerning the collection for the saints, as I have given orders to the churches of Galatia, so you must do also: On the first day of the week let each one of you lay something aside, storing up he may prosper, that there be no collections when I come.

It is so interesting to me that Paul, here and in other letters, is adamant in defending his position to not accept money from churches or to take up special offerings for himself. He applied this same idea to the offerings for the Christians in Judea. Make no mistake; Paul was blessed by many churches he planted and visited, but he was careful about asking for money. But, again, the point here is that tongues did not make the Corinthians more prone to sacrificial giving or bring a prosperous lifestyle.

The reason that speaking in tongues does not do any of the things listed above is very simple: none of these are the purpose of speaking in tongues. Further, as evidenced here, speaking in tongues does not denote spiritual maturity or even correct living, and the believer would be careful to remember that.

Some Cautions About Speaking in Tongues

A young man who works in our church was mentored by a great man of God. Upon his mentor's death there were hundreds at the memorial services who were told that this man's "mantle would fall now" to them. Certainly this is possible; it is even biblical. However, it is a far too frequent occurrence that I see young believers in Christ desperately and legitimately hungering after God in a way that is, simply stated, futile, for they hunger after a blessing, calling, or gifting like that of their mentor (or, in many cases, their idol) when God has a special and unique calling for them. It is important that we develop an understanding about speaking in tongues and exercise some important cautions.

First, do not expect all to operate in the same gifts in the same way. In 1 Corinthians 12:22–31 Paul clearly teaches that all do not receive the same gifts, nor do they operate with the same manifestations:

> No, much rather, those members of the body which seem to be weaker are necessary. And those members of the body which we think to be less honorable, on these we bestow greater honor; and our unpresentable parts have greater modesty, but our presentable parts have no need. But God composed the body, having given greater honor to that part which lacks it, that there should be no schism in the body, but that the members should have the same care for one another. And if one member suffers, all the members suffer with it; or if one member is honored, all the members rejoice with it. Now you are the body of Christ, and members individually. And God has appointed these in the church: first apostles, second prophets, third teachers, after that miracles, then gifts of healings, helps, administrations, varieties of tongues. Are all

apostles? Are all prophets? Are all teachers? Are all workers of miracles? Do all have gifts of healings? Do all speak with tongues? Do all interpret? But earnestly desire the best gifts. And yet I show you a more excellent way.

"You are the body of Christ, and members individually." What an amazing thing! I might not be the healer my mentor was, but I can be what God has called me to be by allowing the Holy Spirit living within me to activate not only the gift but also my zeal for its use.

Second, let your speaking in tongues serve the body of Christ in love. As I have pointed out in an earlier chapter, tongues is useless noise without true, unconditional serving love. These verses are so often quoted that we are apt to dismiss them as truths with which we are already too familiar, but it is appropriate to hear the words of 1 Corinthians 13:1–2 again:

> Though I speak with the tongues of men and of angels, but have not love, I have become sounding brass or a clanging cymbal. And though I have the gift of prophecy, and understand all mysteries and all knowledge, and though I have all faith, so that I could remove mountains, but have not love, _I am nothing._
>
> —EMPHASIS ADDED

It is good for us at this time to reflect on this word _love._ It is not the neat, flowers-and-candy, "I'll never offend you" emotion that is so often incorrectly portrayed as love, but it is instead a godly, passionate love for not just those with whom we are in agreement but also those with whom we would fervently disagree. This agape gives us boldness to speak the truth but to do so in love.

Third, we must honestly admit that tongues is inferior to the prophetic gift. There is much emphasis placed on speaking in tongues by various segments of the church, but Paul was clear in 1 Corinthians 14:1–3 that prophecy was a more important focus:

> Pursue love, and desire spiritual gifts, but especially that you may prophesy. For he who speaks in a tongue does not speak to men but to God, for no one understands him; however, in the spirit he speaks mysteries. But he who prophesies speaks edification and exhortation and comfort to men.

A pastor friend of mine once said, "God made tongues the first gift because it's easier to wrap your head around tongues than it is prophecy." I don't know if that was God's motivation, but the idea makes sense. Speaking in tongues is both a blessing from God *and* an act of faith on the part of believers, who must, in faith, open their mouth and move their lips and believe that God has granted them this gift. However, when we look again at what Paul says here, we see that tongues is not a language that is directed to man but is instead a *God-focused* language. It is clear that God wants to communicate to the church His *now* word in a language they can understand.

Fourth, tongues should be practiced according to scriptural order. You need to read 1 Corinthians 14:6–19 carefully to see that Paul viewed the misuse of tongues as a serious, disruptive problem that hindered evangelism and mission.

For the purposes of space, I want to focus on just a few verses from this section. First, in order to establish the magnitude of this in Paul's view, let's look at 1 Corinthians 14:16–19:

> Otherwise, if you bless with the spirit, how will he who occupies the place of the uninformed say "Amen" at your giving of thanks, since he does not understand what you say? For you indeed give thanks well, but the other is not edified. I thank my God I speak with tongues more than you all; yet in the church I would rather speak five words with my understanding, that I may teach others also, than ten thousand words in a tongue.

Think for a moment on the sheer magnitude of that statement. To give some sense of scope, let's make a comparison.

On November 8, 1857, at New Park Street Chapel in Southwark, London, the great preacher C. H. Spurgeon delivered one of his most famous sermons, "A Call to the Unconverted." This great expositor of God's Word spoke to a congregation of approximately six thousand people and gave a great evangelistic call. The transcript of this sermon has a word count of just under seven thousand words. Paul said that it was more profitable to speak something along the lines of "Jesus Christ died for you!" in a language he understood than to speak over them in tongues at better than the equivalent of Spurgeon's sermon.

None of this is to say that tongues are not important, but again, tongues must function in order. Listen to this wonderful promise found in 1 Corinthians 14:23–25 that Paul illustrates for us if we will follow this model:

> Therefore if the whole church comes together in one place, and all speak with tongues, and there come in those who are uninformed or unbelievers, will they not say that you are out of your mind? But if all prophesy, and an unbeliever or an uninformed person comes in, he is convinced by all, he is convicted by all. And thus the secrets of his heart are revealed; and so, falling down on his face, he will worship God and report that God is truly among you.

Fifth, selfish use of tongues indicates an immaturity and lack of spiritual wisdom. Listen to Paul again in 1 Corinthians 14:26:

> How is it then, brethren? Whenever you come together, each of you has a psalm, has a teaching, has a tongue, has a revelation, has an interpretation. Let all things be done for edification.

In Corinth, some of the believers were showing up, and everyone had "a word from the Lord." God can give a word, to be sure, but Paul was able to discern that the true motivation behind these "words" was a desire to be seen in a kind of "saintly spotlight."

Sixth, speaking in tongues should never "take over" a service. The order set by the Holy Spirit as revealed to the pastor and elders should be followed. Tongues publicly given as prophecy must be interpreted. In 1 Corinthians 14:27–28 Paul wrote:

> If anyone speaks in a tongue, let there be two or at the most three, each in turn, and let one interpret. But if

there is no interpreter, let him keep silent in church,
and let him speak to himself and to God.

This is a simple thing to understand when we read later in
1 Corinthians 14:40 that all things are to be done "decently
and in order."

Seventh, speaking in tongues without regard to biblical
order can be disruptive. Here we tread again into a prickly
patch of church doctrinal history. Let's take a look at 1 Corinthians 14:34–35 before we proceed:

Let your women keep silent in the churches, for they
are not permitted to speak; but they are to be submis-
sive, as the law also says. And if they want to learn
something, let them ask their own husbands at home;
for it is shameful for women to speak in church.

First, let's get some historical context. In the Greek gath-
erings, the women often sat in a balcony-like area while their
husbands sat or stood on the floor closer to the one teaching
or preaching. As a result of their distance, the wives (this
word is important later) and other women often could not
hear what was said, and so they would speak out! That wasn't
the end of the issue. Often the men would engage these
women, either by telling them to be quiet or answering their
questions, and so across-the-room conversations would break
out, and the next thing you know, there's no order.

Before we leave this issue, I believe it would be distracting
to the reader if I did not address this controversial teaching
that women "must be silent in the church" as well as what

I believe to be an issue of translation. First, let's look at the phrase "Let your women."

The two words of importance here are *your* and *women*. The word *your* is the Greek word *humo'n*. It is in the genitive case, which means here, and most often though not always, that it modifies another noun as an indicative of possession. This word translated "women" in the Greek is *gune'*, and it does not, in its truest sense, mean women; it means "wives." Paul then is addressing a relational issue and not a gender issue.

Now, the real crux of this verse we find in the phrase "for they are not permitted to speak." The word translated "for" literally means "because," the implication being that the statement Paul is about to make is a rationale for what he has just said and not a declaration unto itself. The word *permitted* is best translated as "to allow, or suffer." The sense here is that Paul is giving a directive not that women are forbidden in general to speak in churches, but that they should not be allowed to speak—in the interruptive, disorderly manner mentioned before—in the way that they were in Corinth. They were not to speak during the church services without their husband's permission, not due to inferiority but due to the logistics of order! Paul exhorted them to, by all means, question their husband when they got home if they didn't understand something, but don't hinder preaching and evangelism through a disregard for order.

Most importantly, we must understand that Paul never restricted women from ministry. In 1 Corinthians 11:5–10 he gave specific instructions about how they were to comport themselves while praying (the inference is taking a lead in corporate prayer) or prophesying:

> But every woman who prays or prophesies with her head uncovered dishonors her head, for that is one and the same as if her head were shaved.

In Greek culture the woman with a shorn head was a prostitute not under the authority of a husband. Therefore, women who would pray or preach needed their hair as a sign of purity and that they were under the leadership of their husband. It is important to state that this cultural restriction is not in force today, but the principle of faithful marriage and pure living remain.

Eighth, we are to beware of demonic counterfeits. We must be aware that demons can counterfeit tongues. Just as people can be influenced by demons to make false professions of faith, so can Satan transform himself to appear as a minister of righteousness (2 Cor. 11:13–15).

All of these cautions should not hinder the authentic use of tongues by believers. The church should welcome heavenly language as a vital evidence of true spiritual life.

CHAPTER ELEVEN
Speaking in Tongues as Hope for Spiritual Awakening

THERE ARE CLEAR warnings in Scripture about interfering with the work of the Holy Spirit. In 1 Thessalonians 5:19 we read, "Do not quench the Spirit." I like the Living Bible's version of the same verse: "Do not smother the Spirit's fire." The Greek word translated *quench* means "to extinguish a flame" and "to stifle or suppress."

The church in North America for the most part has quenched the Holy Spirit with some notable exceptions. When an unusual movement of God breaks out, some rejoice, but most investigate and criticize.

When our Lord Jesus Christ opened His ministry at Nazareth, His hometown, He announced the yoke-breaking anointing of the Holy Spirit. (See Luke 4:16–30; Isaiah 61:1–2.) The people of Nazareth rejected Jesus's anointed message and sought to push Him off a cliff! When you examine the passage in Luke, you discover Jesus announced the work of the Holy Spirit and the end of racial division. He infuriated his old friends by pointing to Elijah's ministry to a Gentile woman in Zarephath and Elisha's miracle for Naaman the Syrian. They were outraged and offended, so they slandered Him, calling Jesus "Joseph's son" (Luke 4:22). They knew the story of Mary's angelic visit and Jesus's virgin birth. The facts are they hated the supernatural, and they were closed to outsiders.

The rebirth of Pentecostalism and speaking in tongues began in an interracial group. Consequently there were and are elements of racism, denominational pride, and cultural separatism that feed the opponents of the movement. Today, speaking in tongues has moved across the tracks and now is on Main Street!

This is hard for those who view church as a nice group of middle-class and upper-middle-class white people. When the Holy Spirit comes, all the walls must come down. Furthermore, the Holy Spirit will not be harnessed or housebroken by anyone. The Spirit who hovered over the waters at Creation was the same Spirit who released the birth of the church. The church was born as the outpost of another world, with values, miracle-working powers, and its own language! John's announcement was a baptism with the Holy Spirit and fire (Luke 3:16). On the Day of Pentecost, wind, fire, and speaking in tongues heralded the arrival of God's fresh presence on Earth.

The Holy Spirit can be grieved, lied to, and blasphemed, but He will not be ignored. Furthermore, the Holy Spirit will upset all human order. Adam's dead flesh cannot stand the presence of the Holy Spirit. Satan fears, mocks, intimidates, and finally imitates the Holy Spirit. A move of the Spirit of God according to the Word of God is Satan's greatest fear. The great denominations are appointing committees about church resurgence, but no human plan can replace the power of the Holy Spirit. Paul's ministry was marked by a "demonstration of the Spirit and of power" (1 Cor. 2:4). Listen to this admonition Paul gave in Galatians 3:1–5 (NIV):

> You foolish Galatians! Who has bewitched you? Before your very eyes Jesus Christ was clearly portrayed as crucified. I would like to learn just one thing from you: Did you receive the Spirit by observing the law, or by believing what you heard? Are you so foolish? After beginning with the Spirit, are you now trying to attain your goal by human effort? Have you suffered so much for nothing—if it really was for nothing? Does God give you his Spirit and work miracles among you because you observe the law, or because you believe what you heard?

Look at that word *bewitched*. Paul here gives a dire warning to the Galatian assembly that a retreat from the supernatural gifts of God back to dead religion was tantamount to witchcraft!

Like Samson, the church has been shorn of its power and now staggers blindly from program to program hoping for a reversal of the grave they are slowly sliding into! Where are the leaders who will cry out to God as Gideon did in Judges 6:13?

> Gideon said to Him, "O my lord, if the LORD is with us, why then has all this happened to us? And where are all His miracles which our fathers told us about, saying, 'Did not the LORD bring us up from Egypt?' But now the LORD has forsaken us and delivered us into the hands of the Midianites."

If the leaders will not rise up and pray, what are we to do? Will we endure dead religion, faith without power, or a works-based philosophy to give our lives meaning? No! We must seek after God's full anointing and presence, lest we be "delivered into the hands" of our old, dead existence.

Times of Refreshing

Several years ago I was fasting and praying alone in a cabin on a mountain. I woke up and looked at the small electric clock next to my bed, which read 3:19 a.m. The Holy Spirit quickened me to get up and open the Bible to Acts 3:19–21.

> Repent therefore and be converted, that your sins may be blotted out, so that times of refreshing may come from the presence of the Lord, and that He may send Jesus Christ, who was preached to you before, whom heaven must receive until the times of restoration of all things, which God has spoken by the mouth of all His holy prophets since the world began.

Here is a clarion call to change (repentance) accompanied by a promise of refreshing from God's presence. Furthermore, the text implies that there must be a restoration of all the prophetic promises of God before Jesus will return to the earth. Hearers must receive Jesus until the End Time outpouring and restoration.

Recently a noted evangelical leader and pastor of one of the most prestigious historical churches in America confessed privately to me, "If the charismatic gifts, including tongues, ever ceased, they must be restored prior to the Second Coming."

Are the charismatic gifts, including tongues, necessary for the End Time awakening? I believe that the Scriptures declare this clearly. Let's turn back to 1 Corinthians 14:21 (NIV):

> In the Law it is written: "Through men of strange tongues and through the lips of foreigners I will speak to this people, but even then they will not listen to me," says the Lord.

In his discussion on tongues Paul cites Isaiah 28:9–12 as predictive of speaking in tongues and its ministry.

> "Whom will he teach knowledge? And whom will he make to understand the message? Those just weaned from milk? Those just drawn from the breasts? For precept must be upon precept, precept upon precept, line upon line, line upon line, here a little, there a little." For with stammering lips and another tongue He will speak to this people, to whom He said, "This is the rest with which you may cause the weary to rest," and, "This is the refreshing"; yet they would not hear.

This passage declares that God expects more than "precept upon precept" or a well-outlined Bible study. He proposes to speak to the people with "stammering lips and another tongue."

God knew the people needed more than a well-outlined Bible study, as important as that may be. They needed an intimate relationship with Him. God predicts that this is not some foreigner speaking to them but a source of heavenly strength.

Speaking in tongues is God's way of causing "the weary to rest," and, I'll say it again, *speaking in tongues* is "the refreshing." Sadly, those who reject the gift of tongues may know the Bible well, but listen to the prophetic declaration Isaiah makes over them in chapter 28, verse 13:

> But the word of the LORD was to them, "Precept upon precept, precept upon precept, line upon line, line upon line, here a little, there a little," that they might go and fall backward, and be broken and snared and caught.

You see, all the people wanted was something they could understand and explain. All they wanted was "here a little, there a little." The refusal to embrace *all* that God has results in backsliding, falling, becoming ensnared by Satan, and spiritual breakdown.

Jesus's call to the weary in Matthew 11:28–30 promises the gift of rest and a new level of intimate learning.

> Come to Me, all you who labor and are heavy laden, and I will give you rest. Take My yoke upon you and learn from Me, for I am gentle and lowly in heart, and you will find rest for your souls. For My yoke is easy and My burden is light.

The "yoke" of Jesus was the rabbinical prayer shawl called the tallit. *Tallit* means "little tabernacle." Jesus declares the place of rest to be like the prayer shawl over a praying person. It is a place of intimacy like the holy of holies. Jesus promises rest to those who learn from Him. I believe this rest comes as we learn from Him the heavenly languages.

Do not settle for "here a little, there a little." Jesus

promised all of us a life that can be more. Look at Jesus's admonition in Luke 11:13:

> If you then, being evil, know how to give good gifts to your children, how much more will your heavenly Father give the Holy Spirit to those who ask Him!

Notice the promise "how much more will your heavenly Father give *the Holy Spirit* to those who ask Him!" Jesus connects an interesting set of dots here: You are evil (dot 1), and you like to give good things to your children (dot 2), but God (dot 3), who is your heavenly Father (dot 4—also a radical concept for the first-century Jew) will give—a good thing? No, the best thing, which is the Holy Spirit (dot 5), to those who ask (dot 6). It's interesting that Jesus refers to God as "your heavenly Father," implying that He, Jesus, was speaking to all assembled but said that God would give the Holy Spirit *only to those who asked.*

A Final Requirement

What is necessary to receive the gift of tongues? Jesus gave us the one clear simple requirement, and it is found in John 7:37–39:

> On the last day, that great day of the feast, Jesus stood and cried out, saying, "If anyone thirsts, let him come to Me and drink. He who believes in Me, as the Scripture has said, out of his heart will flow rivers of living water." But this He spoke concerning the Spirit, whom those believing in Him would receive; for the Holy Spirit was not yet given, because Jesus was not yet glorified.

Here is a promise that changes your life from a stagnant mud puddle to rivers of clear, fresh, flowing waters!

The condition is simple, "If anyone thirsts, let him come to Me and drink." Simple, is it not? Jesus says: Thirsty? Come and drink! One of those "rivers" could be a prayer language. Will you answer the call?

> Come, Thou Fount of every blessing,
> Tune my heart to sing Thy grace;
> Streams of mercy, never ceasing,
> Call for songs of loudest praise.
> Teach me some melodious sonnet,
> Sung by flaming tongues above.
> Praise the mount, I'm fixed upon it,
> Mount of Thy redeeming love.[1]

CHAPTER TWELVE
Speaking in Tongues and the Heavenly Promise

T HE CRYING WAS over. Jesus had risen in victory over death and the grave! He had appeared to hundreds and was now giving His apostles His last Great Commission.

> Then He said to them, "These are the words which I spoke to you while I was still with you, that all things must be fulfilled which were written in the Law of Moses and the Prophets and the Psalms concerning Me." And He opened their understanding, that they might comprehend the Scriptures. Then He said to them, "Thus it is written, and thus it was necessary for the Christ to suffer and to rise from the dead the third day, and that repentance and remission of sins should be preached in His name to all nations, beginning at Jerusalem. And you are witnesses of these things. Behold, I send the Promise of My Father upon you; but tarry in the city of Jerusalem until you are endued with power from on high."
>
> —LUKE 24:44–49

Look at that! Jesus told the disciples exactly what He wanted them to do, gave them a brief glimpse of the scope of it, and then told them to wait! How often have you had an urging from God that was held in check by a prompting to "be still and know"?

But Jesus was not being capricious in this situation. He conveyed the enormity of the task and then informed His disciples that, as they lacked the ability to complete the task, He was going to send the Holy Spirit, "the Promise of [His] Father" on them, and they would then receive power. That was the "missing ingredient" in the Great Commission. The disciples needed the power found in that promise.

At least six times in the New Testament the coming of the Holy Spirit is called "the promise." You will note that Jesus instructed the disciples not to begin their mission until they had received "the Promise" (Acts 1:4).

Some have said that this promise was simply for the early church. They say, "The fullness of this promise does not continue until our day, and only part of the promise is now available." However, this is not what Scripture says. Let's look at Acts 2:38–39 and read the words of Peter in his great Pentecostal sermon:

> Then Peter said to them, "Repent, and let every one of you be baptized in the name of Jesus Christ for the remission of sins; and you shall receive the gift of the Holy Spirit. For the promise is to you and to your children, and to all who are afar off, as many as the Lord our God will call."

The verb *is* is present active indicative. This means that the promise spoken of here by Peter continues to this present moment! Let's look at the Bible's description of the promise.

You Can Be Endued With Power

Even in the most contemporary of translations, we are sometimes faced with the old linguistic problem of a word or
phrase getting "lost in translation." We might find a word
is translated correctly but loses some of its original power.
Such is the case I think when we look at Luke 24:49 and we
encounter the word *endue*.

> Behold, I send the Promise of My Father upon you;
> but tarry in the city of Jerusalem until you are endued
> with power from on high.

The word *endue* here can mean "in" or "gifted" as in "you
will be gifted with power," or "power from on high will be in
you."

Our word *endowment* comes from this word. If a school
receives an endowment, that means it has received a large
deposit that goes on paying interest and income. When the
promise came on Pentecost, it left a powerful endowment
that is inexhaustible! This word can also mean "quality" or
"ability." The promise speaks to our new qualities and abilities as given and directed by the Holy Spirit.

The word *endued* is often translated "clothed." When I get
up to get dressed in the morning, I choose my clothes with
some care. I want to look nice. I want to make sure that my
clothes are clean and appear the way they should. They are,
after all, the first thing a person will notice about me. The
point here is not that we should give great concern to the per-
ceptions of others. It is simply to illustrate the idea of being
clothed with the Holy Spirit. Literally, the idea is that we

"put on" the Holy Spirit, and He is so active in us that others see Him in us before they see us.

The Promise Is to the Church

Let's look at Acts 1:4 and take note of a very significant word:

> And being *assembled* together with them, He commanded them not to depart from Jerusalem, but to wait for the Promise of the Father, "which," He said, "you have heard from Me."
>
> —EMPHASIS ADDED

They were assembled. The entire "assembly" was to wait for the gift of the Holy Spirit, and, indeed Acts records that on the Day of Pentecost all were filled and blessed with the gift of tongues. But is this important today?

We have made mention previously that the Holy Spirit's visitation on Pentecost was for the purpose of infilling and empowering. Literally, it is God's Spirit living inside the believer. Recall the wonderful revelation made by Paul in Romans 8:11:

> But if the Spirit of Him who raised Jesus from the dead *dwells in you*, He who raised Christ from the dead will also give life to your mortal bodies through His Spirit who dwells in you.
>
> —EMPHASIS ADDED

What a wondrous and glorious thing! The Holy Spirit in Jesus raised Him from the dead, and that *same Spirit* lives now in us! What wondrous things must have been prepared for the church to do! We shouldn't be surprised, though, if we remember Jesus's own words:

> Most assuredly, I say to you, he who believes in Me,
> the works that I do he will do also; and greater works
> than these he will do, because I go to My Father.
> —JOHN 14:12

While some doubt that the miracles of Jesus ever happened, the Spirit-filled and empowered believer has within the power to do, when following the will of our heavenly Father, greater miracles than those of Jesus!

The Promise Is to the Family

It is without question that the family is under attack from all sides in our society. Divorce rates are growing. The lie of premarital cohabitation spreads throughout young (and older) people outside the church *and* in, while dissension between spouses grow and is put on display for the children who, in turn, foster dissent toward their parents. The so-called "generation gap" has never seemed more real than today when there seems to be an unspannable chasm fixed between parents and their children.

It is not God's will that situations like these continue, so He sent the Holy Spirit to perform a miracle in the hearts and souls of believers Let's look at the wonderful prophecy from the Old Testament—the last recorded prophecy from that time—found in Malachi 4:5–6.

> Behold, I will send you Elijah the prophet before the
> coming of the great and dreadful day of the LORD.
> And he will turn the hearts of the fathers to the chil-
> dren, and the hearts of the children to their fathers,
> lest I come and strike the earth with a curse.

In Matthew 11:14 Jesus pointed out that John the Baptist was "the Elijah who is to come." And what was John's message? Yes, it was a message calling for repentance, but the one recorded prophecy of John was, as we have stated, "[Jesus] will baptize you with the Holy Spirit and with fire." So, the work of the Elijah who was to come was to prophesy of the Messiah and of the Holy Spirit; it is through that ministry that the hearts of the sons (children) are turned to their fathers (parents). It is only through the life-transforming work of the Holy Spirit that this miracle can happen.

The Promise Is to All Who Will Answer the Call

This is not the place for a discussion on election, but it is worth pointing out the wonderful statement that God is "not willing that any should perish but that all should come to repentance" (2 Pet. 3:9). This is a mighty and wondrous thing! Salvation requires nothing but our acceptance of Christ's sacrifice and a surrender of our will to His (even the latter is a continuing work). Therefore, if one is a believer, then the promise is available. Look once again at the colossal statement made in Acts 2:39 that emphasizes this great truth:

> For the promise is to you and to your children, and to all who are afar off, as many as the Lord our God will call.

The word *call* means "to summon to oneself." The Holy Spirit is God on the earth calling us into His presence! How greatly this magnifies the meaning of the old hymn.

> Softly and tenderly Jesus is calling,
> Calling for you and for me;
> See, on the portals he's waiting and watching,
> Watching for you and for me.
> Come home, come home;
> Ye who are weary come home;
> Earnestly, tenderly, Jesus is calling,
> Calling, O sinner, come home![1]

The Promise Included the Blessing of Abraham

As mentioned previously, our modern notion of family has been drastically modified from God's intent. We look at things like a birthright inheritance as a charming or quaint Middle Eastern social custom, when, in fact, it was a principle handed down from God to illustrate a great spiritual truth. When the father gave that blessing to his son, it gave the son standing in the community, authority over the father's possessions, and power to speak in the father's name.

God made a covenant promise with Abraham that included specific blessings. Look at Galatians 3:13-14 and see what Paul says has happened to the Abrahamic blessing:

> Christ has redeemed us from the curse of the law, having become a curse for us (for it is written, "Cursed is everyone who hangs on a tree"), that the blessing of Abraham might come upon the Gentiles in Christ Jesus, that we might receive the promise of the Spirit through faith.

When you look at Abraham you see the blessing of:

+ An open heaven
+ Land and possession
+ Angelic activity
+ Victory in war
+ Miracles (birth of Isaac)

Peter, the great transformed preacher of Pentecost, wrote about the promise in the introductory verses of his second letter.

> Simon Peter, a servant and apostle of Jesus Christ, to those who through the righteousness of our God and Savior Jesus Christ have received a faith as precious as ours: Grace and peace be yours in abundance through the knowledge of God and of Jesus our Lord. His divine power has given us everything we need for life and godliness through our knowledge of him who called us by his own glory and goodness. Through these he has given us his very great and precious promises, so that through them you may participate in the divine nature and escape the corruption in the world caused by evil desires.
> —2 PETER 1:1–4, NIV

Look at what this promise includes.

Divine power

The words here in Greek are *Theos dunamis*—literally, the power of God. That is what gives us, according to the Holy

Spirit as revealed to Peter, everything we need that will lead us to a full and abundant life of godliness!

Supernatural gifting

All good gifts are from our Father in heaven! They are, therefore, supernatural even though they might function *in* the natural. These gifts exist as part of the "great and precious promises."

Partakers of the divine nature

This is both a lofty way of conveying the same idea as a birthright blessing and, at the same time, a remarkable mystery. Look at the term in Greek: *koino'nos theios phusis.*

Koino'nos means, literally, a sharer or one with whom something is being shared. *Theios*, we have mentioned before, has to do with God, though in this setting it conveys the idea of *godlike*. Finally, *phusis* expresses the idea of something being germinated, as a seed is planted and, when properly watered and nurtured, explodes in a frenzy of creative change. This word is also used to denote lineal descent, as to one who inherently has possession of certain traits or possessions. What this term means, then, is that we, as believers in Christ who embrace the promise of the Holy Spirit, participate in a complete sharing of the divine seed already germinated! The Holy Spirit has planted and fertilized the seed of God's nature, and His nature is now shared with you and the whole church.

The nouns here are *feminine*, which point to the church as the bride of Christ! When we are sharers of the divine nature, we are active members of the body of Christ.

The Promise Includes the Anointing and Sealing

In my book *An Essential Guide to Baptism in the Holy Spirit* I cover the idea of the Holy Spirit as a "seal" in great detail. However, it is worth spending a moment on this blessed truth here. It says in Ephesians 1:13:

> In [Jesus] you also trusted, after you heard the word of truth, the gospel of your salvation; in whom also, having believed, you were sealed with the Holy Spirit of promise.

Look also at 2 Corinthians 1:20–22:

> For all the promises of God in Him are Yes, and in Him Amen, to the glory of God through us. Now He who establishes us with you in Christ and has anointed us is God, who also has sealed us and given us the Spirit in our hearts as a guarantee.

The "sealing" of the Spirit is God's seal of ownership on your life that gives evidence that the heavenly dimension has marked your life. This mark is outward and visible in one's life. The anointing is the word *charisma*, from which we get the words *gifted* and *equipped*. The label *charismatic* also comes from that word. Some think that a charismatic is one who simply jumps around, speaks in tongues, and is prone to emotionalism, but if you truthfully apply the word's original meaning and intent, a charismatic is simply one who displays the outward mark or "seal" of the Holy Spirit in his or her life. That Spirit transforms them by renewing their mind and giving an abundant life. The life of the Spirit now is a guarantee of what is to come!

Will God Keep His Promise?

This is a sincere question. So many believe that they are either too far gone for salvation or, even if God could somehow see fit to look past their sons and redeem them, certainly they have committed sins far too atrocious to receive anything akin to a Holy Spirit promise.

This is a lie from the pit of hell! The promises of God are "yes and amen" from eternity to eternity. However, lest you think these are just the words of some preacher who wants to sell books or fill pews, look at what the Bible says in 1 Kings 8:56 about God and His promise-keeping abilities:

> Blessed be the LORD, who has given rest to His people Israel, according to all that He promised. There has not failed one word of all His good promise, which He promised through His servant Moses.

Not ONE WORD of His promises have ever failed! God will keep every bit of His promises to you and, as Peter said on Pentecost, "to your children, and to all who are afar off, as many as the Lord our God will call."

Furthermore, when you receive Jesus, you get all the promises. Not just some. ALL! There is not a set of promises that apply to people who were born one day and the next day were sitting in a church pew, a set of promises for those who were born to good homes but strayed for a little while and then got their act together, and a set of promises for those who were, in the mind of some, "going to hell on a greased pole." ALL the promises of God are yes and amen in Christ Jesus!

How Do You Release The Promise in Your Life?

Know this promise came to you in Jesus.

For those who are mature believers this might be a given, but it never hurts to say it again and again: Anything good we have, or to which we have access, is made available to us because of Christ's sacrificial death on the cross. It is there that we find the atoning blood that made the massive veil of the holy of holies tear in two, thus ending our separation from God. It is Jesus—only through Him!

Desire "more" in your Christian life.

Let's look at the parable of the unjust judge found in Luke 18:1–8:

> Then He spoke a parable to them, that men always ought to pray and not lose heart, saying: "There was in a certain city a judge who did not fear God nor regard man. Now there was a widow in that city; and she came to him, saying 'Get justice for me from my adversary.' And he would not for a while; but afterward he said within himself, 'Though I do not fear God nor regard man, yet because this widow troubles me I will avenge her, lest by her continual coming she weary men.'" Then the Lord said, "Hear what the unjust judge said. And shall God not avenge His own elect who cry out day and night to Him, though He bears long with them? I tell you that He will avenge them

> speedily. Nevertheless, when the Son of Man comes,
> will He really find faith on the earth?"

Jesus spoke this parable to encourage us to hunger for God and to seek after Him without losing heart. To release this promise, you have to be willing to get desperate.

Come to Jesus for this release.

As I contemplate how to give commentary to this great proclamation from our Savior, I find myself at a loss. Read His words from John 7:37–39:

> On the last day, that great day of the feast, Jesus
> stood and cried out, saying, "If anyone thirsts, let him
> come to Me and drink. He who believes in Me, as the
> Scripture has said, out of his heart will flow rivers of
> living water." But this He spoke concerning the Spirit,
> whom those believing in Him would receive; for the
> Holy Spirit was not yet given, because Jesus was not
> yet glorified.

Are you thirsty? Come to Jesus.

Come in worship and expectation.

We can boldly approach God's throne in worship! We can without fear come to our Abba with supplication and tears! We need not fear anymore. Read Philippians 3:3.

> For we are the circumcision, who worship God in the
> Spirit, rejoice in Christ Jesus, and have no confidence
> in the flesh.

Therefore, come fearlessly before God in the hope of the release of this promise.

- Get on your knees if able.
- Lift up your head in faith.
- Lift up your hands as a child to the Father.
- Lift up praise and hallelujahs to Jesus.
- Listen for a Spirit-given utterance.
- Cooperate with the Holy Spirit.

Above all, be strong and take courage! Fear not! Do not doubt, and do not fear! Know that your language may be very simple at first. Don't dismiss this. It takes a greater act of faith to accept Jesus than to open your mouth and speak. Also, be aware that your manifestation may come as a song in tongues. This is not without precedent. Remember what Paul said in 1 Corinthians 14:15.

> What is the conclusion then? I will pray with the spirit, and I will also pray with the understanding. I will sing with the spirit, and I will also sing with the understanding.

Also remember Ephesians 5:18–19.

> And do not be drunk with wine, in which is dissipation; but be filled with the Spirit, speaking to one another in psalms and hymns and spiritual songs, singing and making melody in your heart to the Lord.

There is no hard and fast rule or concrete way that the Holy Spirit will manifest in you. Just remember that the Holy Spirit is the precious seal of God and that we are partakers of the divine nature. We are children with a birthright blessing that gives us authority to speak in our Father's name.

This can't be overstated. There are those who will try to make this a complicated process. They will tell you that there is a laundry list of to-do items that you must complete before you can even have a hope of salvation, let alone a portion of greater spiritual gifts and works. This is a pharisaical burden, the kind Jesus mentioned in Matthew 23:1–4.

> Then Jesus spoke to the multitudes and to His disciples, saying: "The scribes and the Pharisees sit in Moses' seat. Therefore whatever they tell you to observe, that observe and do, but do not do according to their works; for they say, and do not do. For they bind heavy burdens, hard to bear, and lay them on men's shoulders; but they themselves will not move them with one of their fingers."

At its most simple, the promise is that taste of heaven, the "earnest" (mentioned in my book *An Essential Guide to Baptism in the Holy Spirit*) signifying your portion of inheritance. Don't live your entire Christian experience trying to piece together a life ordained by God only to discover, like Jack Harris in chapter 1, that your life's puzzle is missing a crucial final piece.

Pastor John Osteen asked a seeking lady if she was sure she was saved. "Yes, sir," she said. "I am going to heaven." Osteen then asked, "Would you like a little heaven in you now?" She was then filled with the Spirit and received her prayer language.[2]

> Have you ever felt the power of the Pentecostal fire,
> Burning up all carnal nature, cleansing out all base
>   desire,

Going through and through your spirit, cleansing all
    its stain away?
Oh, I'm glad, so glad to tell you, it is for us all today.

Jesus offers this blest cleansing unto all His children
    dear,
Fully, freely purifying, banishing all doubt and fear.
It will help you, O my brother, when you sing and
    when you pray.
He is waiting now to give it. It is for us all today.

Some have thought they could not live it while they
    dwell on earth below,
But in this they were mistaken, for the Bible tells us
    so.
And the Spirit now is with us; He can keep us all the
    way.
Then by faith why not receive it? It is for us all today.

You may now receive the Spirit as a sanctifying flame
If with all your heart you seek Him, having faith in
    Jesus' name.
On the cross He bought this blessing; He will never
    say us nay.
He is waiting now to give it. It is for us all today.

It is for us all today, if we trust and truly pray.
Consecrate to Christ your all, and upon the Savior
    call.
Bless God, it is for us all today.[3]

NOTES

Book Opening

1. "Waiting for the Promise" by Fanny Crosby. Public domain.

Chapter Three—Speaking in Tongues and Scripture

1. Wayne Grudem, *Systematic Theology* (Grand Rapids, MI: Zondervan, 1994), 1064.

2. Gerhard Kittel, *Theological Word Study of the New Testament* (Grand Rapids, MI: Wm. B. Eerdman's, 1985), cited in PC Study Bible, version 5.2 (Biblesoft).

3. Ibid.

4. Ibid.

5. BlueLetterBible.org, *The Treasury of Scriptural Knowledge*, s.v. "2 Kings 9:11," http://www.blueletterbible.org/study/tsk/tsk .cfm?b=2Ki&c=9&v=11&t=KJV (accessed October 11, 2010).

6. Kittel, *Theological Word Study of the New Testament*.

Chapter Four—Speaking in Tongues and Jesus Christ

1. There are scholars who contend that the Gospel of Mark ends at chapter 16, verse 8: "And going out they fled from the tomb, for terror and bewilderment seized them; and they said nothing to no one, for they were afraid." There are those who would take advantage of this and say that all of Jesus's words regarding the signs that are to "accompany those who believe," such as the casting out of demons, speaking in tongues, or a supposed inability to be harmed by poisonous snakes or lethal drink, are not valid. As this is not the forum to address these issues, I will not take the time or space. However, the reader can be assured that these arguments against the gospel's continuation—and more importantly, the implication of Jesus's words contained therein—fall apart under scrutiny.

Chapter Five—Speaking in Tongues and Church History

1. John MacArthur, *Charismatic Chaos* (Grand Rapids, MI: Zondervan, 1992.

2. Jack Deere, *Surprised by the Power of the Spirit*, (Grand Rapids, MI: Zondervan, 1993).

3. B. B. Warfield, *Counterfeit Miracles* (n.p.: General Books LLC, 2010).

4. As quoted in Mel C. Montgomery, "Tongues Throughout Church History," BrotherMel.com, http://www.brothermel.com/tonguesthroughoutchurchhistory.aspx (used with permission; accessed December 14, 2010).

5. Ibid.

6. Ibid.

7. Ibid.

8. MacArthur, *Charismatic Chaos*, 234.

9. Ron Phillips, *Awakened by the Spirit* (Nashville: Thomas Nelson, 1999), 87–101.

Chapter Six—Speaking in Tongues and the Church

1. Billy Graham, *The Holy Spirit* (Nashville: Thomas Nelson, 2000), 234.

2. Michael Green, *I Believe in the Holy Spirit* (London: Hodder and Stoughton, 1975), 25.

Chapter Seven—Speaking in Tongues and the Individual

1. Gordon Fee, *God's Empowering Presence: The Holy Spirit in the Letters of Paul* (Grand Rapids, MI: Baker Academic, 2009).

Chapter Eight—Speaking in Tongues as Evidence of Spirit Baptism

1. Frank Bartleman, *Another Wave of Revival* (Springdale, PA: Whitaker House, 1982), 32.

Chapter Nine—Speaking in Tongues and Science

1. Benedict Carey, "A Neuroscientific Look at Speaking in Tongues," *New York Times*, November 7, 2006, http://www .nytimes.com/2006/11/07/health/07brain.html?_r=1&scp=2&sq =benedict+carey&st=nyt (accessed January 19, 2011).

2. Ibid.

3. Ibid.

4. Don Campbell, *Mozart Effect* (Quill: New York, 2001), 101.

5. Ibid., 102.

6. Ibid., 103.

7. Ibid., 104.

8. Ibid.

9. Ibid., 214.

10. Ibid., 210.

Chapter Eleven—Speaking in Tongues as Hope for Spiritual Awakening

1. "Come, Thou Fount of Every Blessing" by Robert Robinson. Public domain.

Chapter Twelve—Speaking in Tongues and the Heavenly Promise

1. "Softly and Tenderly" by Will Lamartine Thompson. Public domain.

2. As told to Ron Phillips by Mrs. John Osteen, summer of 2006.

3. "It Is for Us All Today" by Leander L. Pickett. Public domain.

More Foundational Books
From Ron Phillips

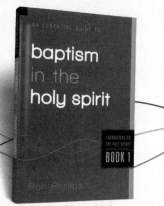

978-1-61638-239-1 / $9.99

Book one in the Foundations on the Holy Spirit explains foundational truths for the Spirit-filled believer and shows how the Holy Spirit works in our lives today.

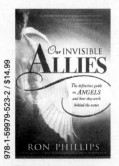

978-1-59979-523-2 / $14.99

The definitive guide on angels and how they work behind the scenes

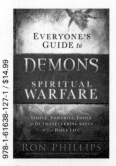

978-1-61638-127-1 / $14.99

Simple, powerful tools for outmaneuvering Satan in your daily life

FREE NEWSLETTERS
TO HELP EMPOWER YOUR LIFE

Why subscribe today?

- ❑ **DELIVERED DIRECTLY TO YOU.** All you have to do is open your inbox and read.

- ❑ **EXCLUSIVE CONTENT.** We cover the news overlooked by the mainstream press.

- ❑ **STAY CURRENT.** Find the latest court rulings, revivals, and cultural trends.

- ❑ **UPDATE OTHERS.** Easy to forward to friends and family with the click of your mouse.

CHOOSE THE E-NEWSLETTER THAT INTERESTS YOU MOST:

- • Christian news
- • Daily devotionals
- • Spiritual empowerment
- • And much, much more

SIGN UP AT: **http://freenewsletters.charismamag.com**

8178